Meeting the Social and Emotional Needs of Gifted and Talented Children

Meeting the Social and Emotional Needs of Gifted and Talented Children

Edited by
Michael J. Stopper

David Fulton Publishers
London

David Fulton Publishers Ltd
Ormond House, 26–27 Boswell Street, London WC1N 3JD

Website: http://www.fultonbooks.co.uk

First published in Great Britain by David Fulton Publishers 2000

Note: The right of Michael J. Stopper to be identified as the editor of this work has been asserted by him in accordance with the Copyright, Designs and Patents Act 1988.

Copyright © David Fulton Publishers 2000

British Library Cataloguing in Publication Data
A catalogue record for this book is available from the British Library

ISBN 1–85346–645–X

Typeset by Elite Typesetting Techniques, Eastleigh, Hampshire
Printed in Great Britain by The Cromwell Press Ltd, Trowbridge, Wilts.

Contents

Notes on contributors

Stan Bailey is a Senior Lecturer in education at the University of New England, Armidale, New South Wales, where he teaches courses in gifted and talented education. He founded the journal *TalentEd* in 1983 and remains its editor. Formerly a primary school teacher, he has been involved extensively in in-service teacher training, works regularly with parent groups and for five years served as a member of the Council of the Australian Association for the Education of the Gifted and Talented.

Richard Bentley was, until recently, Principal Inspector with Worcestershire Local Education Authority, where his brief included coordinating the LEA's provision for pupils of higher ability. Prior to this he was head of a middle school. He has undertaken research in the field and has made study visits and given conference presentations abroad, including a paper at the 11th World Conference in Hong Kong. He has contributed to conferences organised by the National Association for Able Children in Education and is a member of the Editorial Board of the National Association for Gifted Children's journal.

Susan Gomme taught French and Latin after graduating in modern languages. She has seen four children of her own through various stages of formal education – from primary schooling to a variety of postgraduate courses. Since joining the National Association for Gifted Children in 1968, she has worked in many capacities, both local and national. She was a founder member of its Counselling Service (in which she is still active) and recently retired from chairmanship of the association.

Lindsay Peer is Education Director of the British Dyslexia Association. She contributes regularly at both national and international conferences and has published widely. In addition to her role as Vice Chairman of the British Dyslexia Association's Accreditation Board, she is a member of the National Literacy and Numeracy Strategy Groups and has given evidence to House of Commons Select Committees. She has a particular interest in the educational development of bilingual students with learning problems.

Michael J. Stopper is a Local Education Authority Coordinator for Gifted and Able Pupils and previously taught in secondary schools. He is a member of the government's Gifted and Talented Advisory Group and has given evidence on the highly able to a House of Commons Select Committee. His research interests have included provision for the gifted and talented in New South Wales, Australia and he completed his PhD on curriculum enrichment in sixth form colleges. He is a trustee of the National Association for Gifted Children and Chair of its Education and Research Sub-committee.

Belle Wallace has worked with highly able children for 25 years: firstly in an advisory capacity to Essex schools and then as a researcher and developer of a thinking and problem-solving skills base for curriculum development. Since its inception in 1982, she has been editor of the journal *Gifted Education International*. She has published widely and has given keynote presentations at conferences in the UK and throughout the world. Her particular interest and expertise is in working with disadvantaged learners in low socio-economic communities.

Julian Whybra joined the Essex County Working Party for Gifted Children in 1978. From 1985–93 he was the LEA's Advisory Officer for Gifted Education. He later formed GIFT which currently provides over 400 learning extension courses throughout the country and offers training for teachers. He has acted as English Correspondent for the European Council for High Ability (ECHA), is Field Officer for the Gabbitas Truman and Thring Educational Trust's 'Tomorrow's Achievers' Initiative and is a member of the government's Gifted and Talented Advisory Group.

Acknowledgements

I am particularly indebted to Dawn Houtby for her skilful help in the presentation of material at the manuscript stage; to Lincolnshire LEA's English as an Additional Language Team for material cited in Chapter 6, and to all those whose encouragement has helped sustain my enthusiasm for the project. I owe especial thanks to my family who have borne my 'absence' with commendable patience and understanding.

Preface

It is both a privilege and a pleasure to have the opportunity to edit a collection of specially commissioned chapters on the education and personal development of gifted and talented children for this additional contribution to the NACE/Fulton series. It is a task that is infused with a sense of challenge and optimism as a result of new educational horizons, or, perhaps, even closer middle-distance destinations in this developing field.

Though advocacy for the needs of the gifted and talented has been long-established among the few, only recent history has revealed a more common concern and a national impetus for action that is noteworthy by contrast with past inertia. However, an acknowledged, critical aspect of talent development remains under-represented: namely that the principal factors underpinning all learning are social and emotional ones.

Meeting the Social and Emotional Needs of Gifted and Talented Children therefore seeks to highlight the complex relationship between intellectual, social and emotional development that attends notable achievement and individual fulfilment.

The book aims to be of value to anyone concerned with the realisation of high potential: it will, then, I hope, be of equal benefit to parents and to those who educate and nurture in professional settings as well as those who shape policy that governs such processes.

I hope, too, that the book conveys and promotes the idea of needs, not merely as a matter of personal 'adjustment' but as a question of proactive development of social and emotional strengths, for the benefit of the individual and of society. It further recognises the particular contributions of both traditional scientific enquiry and qualitative perspectives; and it brings together a range of authors who have made significant contributions to the field and who, in various contexts of support for gifted and talented children, offer practical guidelines for secure and confident learning. While parts of the book draw on work undertaken in cultural settings other than our own, such commentary offers insights to issues of universal concern.

Finally, a brief note regarding terminology, or 'what's in a name?' The title of this book refers to gifted and talented children; numerous synonyms have existed and continue to exist – chosen historically or presently to avoid perceived 'stereotypical' meanings and associations, for reasons of political expediency and so forth. National debate, action plans and schemes seem set, by government at least, to be carried forward with the given terms of reference; additionally, they have been the currency of much international argument and exposition for some considerable time.

Absolute definitions on the subject continue, unsurprisingly, to elude us: 'high ability' is a point on a continuum and is defined by context – that is to say, it means different things to different people at different times and in different places. The book does not seek to infringe that prerogative; rather it abandons circular debate on nomenclature and definition, in favour of discussing what can be done to help facilitate the development of children's potential, their enjoyment of high achievement and their entitlement to lead happy and fulfilling lives.

Michael J. Stopper
May 2000

The National Association for Able Children in Education

Westminster College, Oxford OX2 9AT

The Association that Helps Teachers Help Able and Talented Children

Aims

- To raise awareness of the particular educational needs which able and talented children have, in order to realise their full potential.
- To be proactive in promoting discussion and debate by raising relevant issues through liaison with educational policy makers.
- To ensure a broad, balanced and appropriate curriculum for able and talented children.
- To advocate the use of a differentiated educational provision in the classroom through curriculum enrichment and extension.
- To encourage commitment to the personal, social and intellectual development of the whole child.
- To make education an enjoyable, exciting and worthwhile experience for the able and talented.

CHAPTER 1

Introduction

Michael J. Stopper

Current interest in the gifted and talented

It is beyond the scope of this book to unfold the extensive historical backcloth to current national interest in, and concern for, the education of gifted and talented children. However, many will welcome the burgeoning literature which supports this and the higher profile which these children now have within the government's educational agenda – driven by the principle of social inclusion. Some of the more recent influences which have given rise to current developments are, none the less clearly apparent; they include: intensive lobbying by national associations working in this field, the critical findings of Her Majesty's Inspectorate (HMI) and the Office for Standards in Education (OFSTED), increased emphasis on both special need and differentiated provision in classrooms and a more discerning stance by parents with regard to mismatches between their children's ability and the level of work they undertake in school. All of this has been interwoven with the enhanced 'newsworthiness' that issues regarding the gifted and talented now seem to have assumed in the media.

However, optimism generated by such developments needs to be tempered by the recognition that the key lead given by government is very much outcomes-focused and less concerned with inputs and procedures, i.e. with strategy. In particular, we are left to infer how to equip and enskill gifted and talented children within the social and emotional dimensions of learning.

The social and emotional foundations of learning

It has taken a considerable period of time for due consideration to be given to the effects of social and emotional development on knowing and thinking and understanding. As psychological inquiry has advanced (e.g. Hoffman 1986) we have come to accept the closeness of the relationship with greater certainty, although intuitive perceptions of it have long-existed (Stednitz 1995). Additionally, within the structure of the brain itself, we have the biological indicators to reinforce theory, intuition and observational study: its hemispherical architecture which respectively denotes functioning that is cognitive or more affective (left brain/right brain) in character, also features a greater array of inter-connecting 'information pathways' between the hemispheres than is found between the brain and any other area of the body.

In its potential for promoting effective learning, such knowledge has found a comfortable identity in integrated approaches to education such as that developed by Clark (1988). This embraced the premise that thinking, feeling, intuitive and physical sensing functions were interdependent, mutually reinforcing prerequisites for successful learning and living. The social and emotional underpinning of and interplay with effective learning has been similarly discussed by Butler-Por (1987), George (1992), Wallace and Adams (1993), Webb (1993), Lubinski (1993) and Landau and Weissler (1998) among others.

Socio-emotional constituents of definitions and models

While some authorities in the field have focused on the cognitive components of high ability, we can trace the evolution of alternative and, essentially, broader conceptions of giftedness and talent. Such insights were evident over 80 years ago when William Stern recognised that factors other than high intelligence were necessary for outstanding achievement. These factors, he suggested, included motivation and an appropriate environment (Stern 1916).

Although Terman (1925–9) had conducted research on the basis of a firm belief in intelligence as a unitary trait that was genetically determined and chronologically stable, his position was modified as a result of the later empirical data of his own genetic studies. These led him to conclude that many of his subjects had never made use of their 'superior' ability and (foreshadowing subsequent developmental theories) that factors other than intelligence fundamentally affect an individual's 'life success'. Renzulli's (1977) model of giftedness reflected this concern for the inclusion of non-intellective factors. His 'three-ring conception' incorporated the trait of task commitment in addition to creativity and above average ability. In the analysis of task commitment we are able to note essential elements that are central to the concerns of this book. These include: high levels of interest and enthusiasm, sustained effort, self-confidence and self-belief and comfortable accommodation of self-criticism and the criticism of others.

Further development of the trait-orientated approach to theories of giftedness came with the work of Gardner (1983). His taxonomy of seven distinct intelligences has had a significant impact on the identification of talent and on consideration of the means by which it might best be nurtured. Of especial interest in any examination of the social and emotional determinants of high performance is Gardner's proposition of intrapersonal (understanding of self) and inter-personal (understanding of others) intelligences.

Gagné's (1991) 'Differentiated Model of Giftedness and Talent', which distinguished a correspondence to aptitude in respect of giftedness and a correspondence to performance in respect of talent, gave added weight to acknowledgement of social and emotional factors. Gagné included socio-affective aptitudes within the five domains that he proposed, though later commenting (Gagné 1993) that the exploration of sub-categories within this extensive area was still relatively limited. Among pro-social abilities that were likely to be included, however, Gagné notes empathy or understanding of the views and feelings of others and social influence. The model further specifies two distinctive catalysts that act upon the aptitudes and their application in acquiring knowledge and skills, in order for talent(s) to emerge: the two types of catalyst are intra-personal and environmental.

With regard to the intra-personal catalysts, recognition is given to the importance of Renzulli's motivational component and to personality characteristics. The environmental catalysts are represented as 'significant factors' which relate to persons, places, interventions, events and chance. Of these, Gagné highlights the critical impact on talent development made by significant individuals such as parents and family members, teachers and other adult role models.

The extended consideration given here to Gagné's model, ought to signal its suggested value in helping us to understand the interactive relationship between social, emotional and cognitive development and the means by which potential may be translated into performance.

In concluding this selective review of emerging social and emotional dimensions of giftedness and talent, it seems appropriate to note the 'radical' position of an author whose work propelled him to the top of a UK non-fiction 'best-seller' book-list. Daniel Goleman (1996) regards emotional intelligence as the key to effective thinking and decision-making processes – a 'master aptitude': one which can be taught; which is able to be regulated by the individual and one which promotes wide-ranging personal success. In offering a redefinition of more traditional notions of intelligence, Goleman argues that those qualities prerequisite for such success include self-awareness, impulse control, persistence, empathy and social dexterity.

Thus we can establish the consensus that social and emotional well-being is the seed of effective learning; what remains is the challenge of seeing this fully translated in terms of educational policy and process and within family and community life.

ISOLATION —

The concept of 'needs'

The concept of 'needs' has a pivotal place within this book. It is important, therefore, I feel, for us to consider how needs might be derived and how they might be assessed or interpreted. 'Need' seems a common enough idea for us to easily assume a shared understanding and, consequently, of the kind of process that we might engage in when we seek to meet children's needs. Much of what we read or hear on educational matters certainly creates that impression; yet, as I hope will become evident from the discussion that follows, such assumptions may not be well-founded. One way of thinking about needs can be to represent them in a 'composite' way. One 'set' of needs arises from the combination of characteristics particular to any given child – different from all others to some degree, and a result of the chance alchemy of experience or opportunity, personality, motivation and ability. In schools, such infinite variety will provide the challenge of translating public rhetoric into reality if the needs of individuals are truly to be taken into account.

Other needs can be seen to have their origin in what might be described as an 'affiliation' – shared with those who have similar talents and abilities and which form the basis for grouping strategies that bring such children together for targeted learning experiences. Such an affiliation might be seen as fundamental to the development of a healthy self-concept: in part providing a realistic appraisal of one's talents and offering in parallel, reassurances that one is not isolated in the life challenges to be faced, by virtue of personal interests, or through one's hopes and aspirations.

Finally, recognition can be given to those needs deemed common to all children in order to lead happy and fulfilling lives. The interaction between cognitive, social, emotional, physical and intuitive growth in optimising the development of all individuals, has been conceptualised in Maslow's (1954) 'Hierarchy of Human Needs'. Personal growth is portrayed as progression through the various levels of need which originate in the basic physical requirements that support life, and which lead ultimately to self-actualisation where potential is fully realised and one's true self is discovered. Since Maslow's work is examined in greater detail by Susan Gomme in a later chapter, it is sufficient only to further note here that the model has been referred to increasingly in recent debate about the holistic needs of the gifted and talented and has been viewed as an attractive means of structuring provision both at home and at school.

Needs and gender

We might examine also whether needs are gender specific: that is to say, whether boys and girls are sufficiently distinct in biological terms to merit differentiated support, or if it is the case that social and cultural expectations give rise to a self-fulfilling prophesy in respect of the behaviours that we observe. Space does not permit an extended discussion of this important topic here, but several issues might inform readers' thinking on the matter in the various contexts addressed in the book. If we accept the importance of early learning experiences in the development of high ability, we will be keenly interested in the 'messages' that we give when learning begins. While we may not be conscious of these early cues, there is sufficient evidence (e.g. Fox and Zimmerman 1985) for us to acknowledge the encouragement given to boys in developing qualities of independence and self-reliance and a sense of responsibility. We know, too, that the abilities of girls are likely to be identified later and less often than is the case with boys (Walker *et al.* 1992). As formal education progresses, refuge can be taken in neatness and industry, which affects the judgements teachers make about the quality of work. It is not surprising to find that under-achievement among girls remains undetected more often (McCall *et al.* 1992). Although the pattern of causation is not easy to unravel, it is entirely consistent to discover that girls are more prone than boys to credit their success to external events beyond their control, rather than to the results of their own aptitude (Freeman 1991).

It could be argued that, unless we further consider the provision of appropriate female role models at critical educational stages; help counteract and relieve the particular pressures of peer conformity in adolescence and recognise the need for sensitive and comprehensive career guidance, we may well continue to see the atrophying of talent among half of the population on a widespread scale. Although timely initiatives to narrow the gender gap can be seen to have accelerated girls' level of examination performance beyond that of boys, in all areas of the curriculum, such measures have still to make their indelible mark in the world beyond school, further and higher education. Thus we must continue to reflect on girls' levels of aspiration and self-esteem, as well as upon the opportunities that society affords. While more recent concern for boys' performance in the classroom has become the dominant theme, the success achieved by some male sub-groups gives us a more 'fuzzy' focus, by comparison, on the 'new gender problem'.

Individual needs and societal needs

Another perspective comes from examining the meeting of needs at an individual level and at a societal level (the latter sometimes being distinguished as the needs of society and the needs of the economy). On ideological grounds, we might decide to prioritise one or the other; alternatively, we might come to regard education as the complex business of adapting societally – required ways of gratifying individual needs. Realistically, some might argue, the two are liable to be in continuous conflict; school, after all, could be said to be a prerequisite for living – moulding and nurturing the young according to adult norms and future expectations. This would, conceivably, perhaps, be much at odds with concern for the 'here and now' in life, which presupposes the need to 'Permit children their own individuality, and enjoy them for who they are, not who you would like them to be' (Clark 1988, p. 570). Leyden (1997) demonstrates something of this tension in describing 'Nurturing Communities' which invest for the long term; which 'safeguard' activities that may not offer an immediate return, and which focus on contributions to the 'wholeness of human experience'; and 'Nurturing Schools' that provide learning opportunities which allow individual needs to be met, and which include the pursuit of special interests with like-minded peers.

Do we then have to judge whether needs are short term or long term, or whether they are derived from an unstable amalgam of present and future contexts? Or, might we in a sense be spared such a dilemma if we accept, as Csikszentmihalyi *et al.* (1993) have pointed out, that our capacity as human beings to adapt to future changes and challenges in the world in which we live, is dependent upon a diversity of talents which can be drawn upon as occasion demands? There is an interesting parallel here in the earlier work of Tannenbaum (1983) who proposed a sub-division of developed talents into four categories:

1. 'scarcity' talents, which facilitate the furthering of knowledge and major human accomplishments;
2. 'surplus' talents, that contribute to our aesthetic pleasure in the social environment;
3. 'quota' talents, without which society would be deemed unable to function effectively, and
4. 'anomalous' talents, which include practical skills – those that offer scope for entertainment, abilities that were valued historically and even those of which a society generally disapproves!

In various cultural contexts, or as priorities alter with the passage of time, it is not difficult to envisage a given talent 'coming into its own'. Thus the whole idea of 'talent' and, therefore, of the optimal conditions which will allow it to flourish is, of course, socially constructed. If the seal of approval that we give to particular traits and behaviours takes account of a pool of talent of almost infinite depth, might we have a greater latitude in educating children according to their interests (in the sense of that which interests them) and, consequently, in seeking to meet their individual needs? Harmony of this kind has been summarised by VanTassel-Baska (1993):

At a fundamental level, the gifted develop as individuals in a reciprocal relationship with their society; thus, their creative work carries meaning beyond themselves whether it is fully intended to or not. By the same token, a society is enriched by having individuals actively engaging in self-chosen creative endeavours. (p. 383)

The social environment

In considering the background against which the needs of gifted and talented children are met, we can explore more fully the interaction with the social environment in which they find themselves. There is agreement within the literature on the far-reaching effects of context: Freeman (1996) and Gross (1994) for example, while adopting different positions on the extent to which the intrinsic social and emotional needs of the gifted and talented differ significantly from those of other children, draw attention respectively, to 'behaviours … heavily influenced by circumstances' (Freeman 1996, pp. 76–7) and to 'difficulties (which) lie … in teachers' and classmates' reactions ...' (Gross 1994, p. 9).

There are issues to be addressed here in acknowledging the possible vulnerability of some children, and determining the extent to which individuals may be 'at risk'. Gross depicts a 'forced choice dilemma', where there is a lack of congruence between the values of the individual and the group to which he or she belongs: if intimacy with peers is sought it may be at the expense of individual intellectual and emotional fulfilment; on the other hand, acceptance by the group might be waived in favour of striving for high achievement.

Although Gross argues that psycho-social need is likely to be satisfied in neither instance, we ought, perhaps, to beware of generalisation while being alert to individuals within situations where the potential for under-achievement can exist – therefore taking each case on its merits.

The needs of the creatively gifted and talented

Following a related line of argument, Shore *et al.* (1991) examine the question of curricular or social conformity with particular reference to the creatively gifted and talented. Since creativity (in the sense in which it is used here) and non-conformity have a degree of shared identity, we might anticipate the need to resolve tensions where restrictions are likely to occur. Freeman (1996), for example, notes that creativity is only likely to 'flower' where there is emotional freedom (but that, conversely, emotional restraint may be a prerequisite for high scholastic attainment). A negotiated approach to learning in which adults are comfortable with requests prefaced by: 'Will it be alright if …?', and which allows for the following of personal interests wherever possible, could help maximise creative abilities. However, practical considerations apart, schools and communities are likely to differ widely in the value they attach to personal independence and divergent behaviour. Helping young people to come to terms with the 'system' as necessity demands, may appear to be an inevitable responsibility that both teachers and parents share. Enabling children to develop the skill of adapting their behaviour and to make appropriate choices about 'conforming' to the satisfaction of others in pursuit of their individual goals, might be seen to generally ease their path in life. Such a strategy would then be complemented by the concern for young people to preserve their personal integrity and for home and school environments to offer positive support for their personal identity (Shore *et al.* 1991, p. 239).

Statements of need

As we have seen, then, there are various ways of looking at the idea of needs; furthermore, needs are not obvious or indisputable and consequently, may not necessarily be easily agreed upon. It is important that we are clear about the basis upon which we make statements of need: in arriving at such decisions we may have found apparently comfortable solutions in doing no more than relying on our 'common sense'. Since common sense is, in reality, either just that – a sense of things which is common (though not necessarily more valid as a result) or, alternatively, is synonymous with personal prejudice, might we rely on a more scientific perspective? Where the interpretation and assessment of needs is concerned, knowledge that we might seek in this way ought to be put in its proper context, for this is an evaluative matter, not an empirical one.

This is not the same as suggesting that research into social and emotional predisposition and behaviour is not held to be of value – merely that this will not, of itself, provide us with the 'answers' to children's needs. We should recognise that to say that someone does not have something does not actually provide us with evidence of a need, and that where statements of need are being furnished we have to consider the values that are guiding them. For needs have no existence in abstraction from the valuation of goals, since all needs presuppose the usefulness of the ends they serve. This leaves us in the inescapable position that to speak of meeting a need (whether individual or societal) raises rather than settles questions as to its value.

In choosing to fashion the aims of education through the concept of needs, 'common sense' might suggest that we look for a steer in direction by 'starting from the child'. We have already considered the important role of motivation in talent development and it seems but a short step to conclude that education which starts from the needs of the child will guarantee that critical factor. However, this might only be true to some extent if needs are regarded as synonymous with wants, and plainly, a child may not necessarily want what s/he needs. This is an important distinction, since what drives the individual is a sense of what is important and useful. We are still fondly attached to the notion of education as a process of growth; in tracing that concept back almost a century to its origins, we find that its architect, John Dewey, conceived of it as the enjoying and further development of experiences recognised by us to be valuable (Dewey 1902).

I have not drawn attention to this whole question of needs in order to suggest that, in aiding the social and emotional development of gifted and talented children, we are inevitably beset by insoluble moral and practical problems. I would argue, however, that we can easily 'play a little too fast and loose' with the interpretation and assessment of needs, and that a more critical sensitivity on our part will better serve those whom we wish to support. What follows in this book is properly prefaced, in my view, by that important fact and, therefore, by a recommendation for:

- precision about the goals for which needs are said to be required;
- clarity about the nature of the needs themselves; and
- understanding of their relevance to education, specifically as the means to their satisfaction.

The children in our care deserve no less.

References

Butler-Por, N. (1987) *Underachievers in School*. London: Wiley.

Clark, B. (1988) *Growing Up Gifted*. Columbus, OH: Merrill.

Csikszentmihalyi, M., Rathunde, K. and Wholen, S. (1993) *Talented Teenagers: The Roots of Success and Failure*. Cambridge: Cambridge University Press.

Dewey, J. (1902) *The Child and the Curriculum*. Chicago: University of Chicago Press.

Fox, L. H. and Zimmerman, W. (1985) 'Gifted women', in Freeman, J. (ed.) *The Psychology of Gifted Children: Perspectives on Development and Education*. Chichester: Wiley.

Freeman, J. (1991) *Gifted Children Growing Up*. London: Cassell.

Freeman, J. (1996) 'The early development and education of highly able young children', in Cropley, A. J. and Dehn, D. (eds) *Fostering the Growth of High Ability: European Perspectives*. Norwood, NJ: Ablex Publishing Corporation.

Gagné, F. (1991) 'Toward a differentiated model of giftedness and talent', in Colangelo, N. and Davis, G. A. (eds) *Handbook of Gifted Education*. Boston: Allyn and Bacon.

Gagné, F. (1993) 'Constructs and models pertaining to exceptional human abilities', in Heller, K. A., Mönks, F. J. and Passow, A. H. (eds) *International Handbook of Research and Development of Giftedness and Talent.* Oxford: Pergamon Press.

Gardner, H. (1983) *Frames of Mind.* New York: Basic Books.

George, D. R. (1992) *The Challenge of the Able Child.* London: David Fulton Publishers.

Goleman, D. (1996) *Emotional Intelligence.* London: Bloomsbury.

Gross, M. U. M. (1994) 'Responding to the social and emotional needs of gifted children', *Australasian Journal of Education* **3**(2), 4–10.

Hoffman, M. L. (1986) 'Affect, cognition and motivation', in Sorrentino, R. M. and Higgins, E. T. (eds) *Handbook and Motivation and Cognition: Foundations of Social Behaviour.* Chichester: Wiley.

Landau, E. and Weissler, K. (1998) 'The relationship between emotional maturity, intelligence and creativity in gifted children', *Gifted Education International* **13**(2), 100–5.

Leyden, S. (1997) 'A climate for growth'. Paper presented at the NASEN, NAGC and NACE Annual Study Course: *Unlocking Potential: More Able Children and Their Particular Needs.* Hinckley, Leicester.

Lubinski, D. (1993) Discussion of symposium paper 'The early lives of child prodigies', Howe, M. J. A., in Bock, G. R. and Ackrill, K. (eds) *The Origins and Development of High Ability* (Ciba Foundation Symposium 178). Chichester: Wiley.

Maslow, A. H. (1954) *Motivation and Personality.* New York: Harper and Row.

McCall, R. B., Evahn, C. and Kratzer, L. (1992) *High School Underachievers: What Do They Achieve as Adults?.* London: Sage.

Renzulli, J. S. (1977) *The Enrichment Triad Model: A Guide for Developing Defensible Programs for the Gifted and Talented.* Wethersfield, CT: Creative Learning Press.

Shore, B. M., Cornell, D. G., Robinson, A. and Ward, V. S. (1991) *Recommended Practices in Gifted Education: A Critical Analysis.* New York: Teachers College Press.

Stednitz, U. (1995) 'Psychosocial dimensions of talent: some major issues', in Freeman, J., Span, P. and Wagner, H. (eds) *Actualizing Talent: A Lifelong Challenge.* London: Cassell.

Stern, W. (1916) 'Psychologische begabungsforschung und begabungsdiagnose (Psychological research on the gifted and diagnosis of giftedness)', in Peterson, P. (ed.) *Der Aufstieg der Begabten.* Leipzig: Teubner.

Tannenbaum, A. J. (1983) *Gifted Children: Psychological and Educational Perspectives.* New York: Macmillan.

Terman, L. M. (1925–9) *Genetic Studies of Genius*, Vols 1–4. Stanford, CA: Stanford University Press.

VanTassel-Baska, J. (1993) 'Theory and research on curriculum development for the gifted', in Heller, K. A., Mönks, F. J. and Passow, A. H. (eds) *International Handbook of Research and Development of Giftedness and Talent.* Oxford: Pergamon Press.

Walker, B. A., Reiss, S. M. and Leonard, J. S. (1992) 'A developmental investigation of the lives of gifted women', *Gifted Child Quarterly* **36**, 201–6.

Wallace, B. and Adams, H. B. (1993) 'The "Thinking Actively in a Social Context" TASC project: developing the potential of children in disadvantaged communities', in Wallace, B. and Adams, H. B. (eds) *Worldwide Perspectives on the Gifted Disadvantaged.* London: AB Academic Publishers.

Webb, J. T. (1993) 'Nurturing social-emotional development of gifted children', in Heller, K. A., Mönks, F. J. and Passow, A. H. (eds) *International Handbook of Research and Development of Giftedness and Talent.* Oxford: Pergamon Press.

CHAPTER 2

Curriculum development and process in mainstream classrooms

Richard Bentley

Introduction

Assuming that our most able pupils do have particular needs (including a range of social and emotional needs) associated with their high ability, how is the school to make adequate provision? What is the best way for a school to provide? What would be judged to be the best sort of curriculum experience? These are common questions, and ones to which there are no quick and obvious answers. However, all those involved with the most able, from whatever standpoint, do want guidance on what should be provided and do want practical advice on the quality of that provision.

In exploring issues of curriculum development and process in mainstream classrooms, I try to maintain a dual focus on practicality and provision. Observations of the school context are made against the background of a role that takes me regularly into schools of different types and age groupings, and with different management styles. However, I cannot set out to explore every aspect of possible provision in relation to the needs of the most able, nor can I hope to arrive at a blueprint for the ultimate in provision strategy. What I can do is consider the context for provision; the route by which detail of provision will be arrived at; and some of the characteristics of appropriate and successful provision.

While my intention is to be practical, I need to start by rehearsing a theoretical construct which underpins my argument of not being able to point to one single 'best' provision strategy. It concerns the relationship between characteristics, identified needs, and related provision; in particular, the central issue of provision being clearly driven by a proper understanding of need. This is the weak (and sometimes missing) link to which I make later reference.

Much of my consideration of provision goes on to be based within the context of school 'climate'. In this connection, I explore a number of what I regard as features associated with, or indicators of, appropriate climate in terms of the social and emotional needs of the most able. I regard climate in this context as both the sum of the characteristics of provision, and as part of the provision itself. It would be difficult to imagine some aspect of provision genuinely flourishing in a school ethos which was not supportive of the most able and their needs, and which did not actively encourage the development of pupils' thinking skills. The climate may be seen to be very much part of the management role at classroom, subject/department and whole school levels. It doesn't just happen, but needs to be consciously worked at, fostered, and shaped. It is an important and tangible aspect of the overall management of the school.

Positive indicators of climate, which are particularly (though not exclusively) in evidence in the classroom, share the characteristic of flexibility. This is the thread running through the debate on provision supportive of the social and emotional needs of the most able. Indeed, a flexible, tailored approach is the basis of some specific 'packages' of curriculum provision that I summarise towards the end of the chapter.

The weak (and sometimes missing) link

Specific and very real needs, like those outlined in the previous chapter, should logically form the basis for appropriate provision. It seems so obvious! But in the hectic schedule of a school the link between need and provision can be one that is not paid the careful attention it deserves. We have already seen that the needs themselves are based upon the characteristics of the able child – the able child in general, the able mathematician (or whatever) if we are considering subject-specific high ability, and our own knowledge and understanding of each of the individual pupils in question. These characteristics are likely to include those helpfully categorised by Clark (1988) as falling within cognitive, affective, physical, intuitive and societal domains, and to embrace social and emotional elements.

In general, schools are recognised as having become much better at knowing, and understanding the basis of, these characteristics. The numerous very helpful published checklists (between which there is a significant element of match) have supported the development of school awareness in this respect. Examples of such checklists are provided and discussed by Leyden (1998), Eyre (1997), George (1997), and Clark and Callow (1998). In many schools, these lists are being used effectively to support teachers in the identification/recognition of more able pupils, and to sharpen teacher judgements in this process. At the same time, increasing use is being made of subject-specific lists in terms of recognising or confirming high ability in particular areas of the curriculum. Lists of characteristics are likely to be particularly helpful where ability is not readily apparent in terms of academic attainment, or where achievement is masked or confused by behavioural, social or emotional issues.

There is also evidence of general improvement in terms of provision for the most able. A whole range of factors, as has been noted in Chapter 1, have all contributed to a greater awareness of the most able. With this has come an increase, in quantifiable terms, of provision for the most able, though in both cases the picture continues to be an uneven one, and generally less positive in terms of the exceptionally able. Unfortunately, this increased effort and involvement by schools has not always paid off in qualitative terms. In many instances, the quality of provision for the most able reflects neither the increased effort and willingness on the part of those involved, nor their greater understanding of the characteristics of the most able. Too often, this variation in quality between characteristics and recognition on the one hand and provision on the other reflects the fact that insufficient attention is paid to the needs relating to these same characteristics. In the busy context of the school, with the many and varied demands being made upon its time, the particular and often very specific and subtle needs of the most able are too often neither adequately articulated nor taken into account in shaping and refining provision. This applies both to the most able in general and in relation to individual able pupils. Even where needs are properly understood (and, frequently, sympathised with), they are not translated into the detail of provision. This greater awareness, analysis and use of needs in programme development is the weak, and sometimes missing, link! But it is an extremely time-consuming and labour-intensive link, and one which schools will continue to find it difficult to put firmly in place without additional support.

Strengthening the link

A particularly useful and practical exercise with teachers and parents, in terms of helping to strengthen this link (or, at least, ensure that it is given due attention) and so relate provision to need, is outlined below. Essentially, it involves those concerned in making a series of 'matches' on a three-column chart:

Column one

- First, consider the characteristics exhibited by an individual pupil (or perhaps group, though this inevitably will lead to less precision). Use 'text book' characteristics in published lists as a starting point, either including, abandoning or amending them as appropriate. This is the first match – that of 'standard' anticipated characteristics to individual 'real' characteristics.

- The debate in this exercise is important in distinguishing the reality of the individual from the potential caricature of the norm. It is the stage at which subtleties of individual characteristic will be introduced.
- At the same time, be wary of seeing these characteristics as necessarily fixed. Consider the extent to which they are already shaped by social and emotional experience/a received education package, and the extent to which they might be influenced by future planned experience. It is useful, therefore, to annotate the characteristics with examples of relevant behaviour.

Column two

- Taking this set of characteristics, characteristic behaviour and previous experience (or lack of it), next consider what particular needs the individual has in terms of future provision.
- In terms of the individual child, there is the potential to be specific. Effectively, this will form the basis of an individualised programme of provision.

Column three

- Proposed provision that matches the agreed needs of the second column is added.
- This will relate to issues of both appropriate curriculum experiences and curriculum modification in content terms. It will also address issues of organisation and approach.
- It will also take cognisance of the broader aspects of provision to support individualised development, including social and emotional considerations.
(see Figure 2.1, p.16)

So, the three-column model will look like this (see Figure 2.2, p.20):

As an example of the model in practice, I have completed a set of columns in terms of Pupil X, a hypothetical able pupil of indeterminate age and gender. This indetermination inevitably results in later lack of precision, particularly in column three. However, I hope that it serves to illustrate the potential of the exercise in shaping curriculum provision.

The characteristics I have selected for Pupil X are typically associated with high ability and are based on the tables of differentiating characteristics within the cognitive and affective domains identified by Clark (1988). The clutch of inter-related characteristics chosen have in common a significance in terms of the pupil's operation within a social/learning context. They have a particular relevance to everyday relationships – with fellow pupils, teachers and other adults – within the classroom and the wider school community, and also with parents in terms of the extended school day. There is, therefore, a significant relevance in terms of the climatic issues under consideration.

I have annotated the list in column one (using italics) to show how what might be seen as characteristic strengths have, in the case of Pupil X, in some instances started to have negative implications in terms of reported behaviour. These could become the basis of future problems if not addressed by a careful analysis of need and thoughtful suggestions for a targeted provision programme (as shown in columns two and three respectively).

Figure 2.1 Some differentiating characteristics relating to pupil X

Column one: Some differentiating characteristics relating to pupil X, together with notes on practical examples of behaviour related to the characteristics and which cause a degree of concern (and will be reflected in the related provision).

- **An evaluative approach to self and others; high expectations of self and others; thinks critically; self-critical:**
  * *sometimes impatient with other less able members of the class*
  * *instances of obvious impatience with the teacher*
  * *tends to be a perfectionist*
  * *has on occasion got very discouraged over own efforts that s/he judges to have fallen short of her/his envisaged end product*

- **Enjoys organising things, and people, into structure or order; seeks to develop systems, strategies, rules; these may be especially complicated:**
  * *sometimes comes across as 'bossy' – there have been occasions when other pupils have complained of this*
  * *other children sometimes don't understand complex plans – recent difficulty over invented game when the rest of the group did not understand the rules*

- **Idealism and strong sense of justice and what is fair; love of truth, equity and fair play; strong interest in current/world affairs, and matters of great importance:**
  * *recently upset after seeing TV pictures of famine victims*
  * *raised issue of food surpluses in Western world*

- **Independent, preferring individualised work; reliant on self; conventional approach to some work; creative and inventive, enjoying new ways of doing things:**
  * *sometimes doesn't find it easy to work with peers*

- **Thinking in alternatives and abstract terms; sensing and appreciating consequences; making generalisations, and visualising solutions.**

Column two: Related needs of pupil X.

- Opportunities to recognise own strengths and weaknesses, as well as those of others.

  To learn to set realistic goals.

  To learn to accept setbacks as part of learning process.

  To learn to make positive use of critical thinking skills.

  Similarly, to make positive use of self-critical ability and also, 'balancing'; experience in creative thinking.

- To be involved in a range of organising opportunities – in different fields, of different types and scale, and with different groups of people.

  To be exposed to problems and tasks which require strategy or system development, or clarity of detail in rules/regulations.

  To explore, practise and develop own leadership style which is valued in school community.

- To overcome negative reactions by exploring values to which student is able to be committed.

  To have access to, and opportunity to explore, current affairs/world events.

- Opportunities to work individually, and to explore own strengths/areas for development.

  To understand own strengths and comparative weaknesses.

  To work cooperatively with others.

  Some opportunity for unconventional approaches to be legitimised.

  Opportunity for creativity to be allowed to develop, and to be challenged to support further development.

- To be exposed to alternatives, abstractions, consequences of choices.

  Opportunities for generalising and testing generalisations.

  Opportunities to design solutions, and (again) to predict consequences.

Column three: Related considerations for/suggestions of provision: some organisational and classroom strategies planned to support pupil X.

- Evaluative experience in a range of curricular areas. Opportunity to chair evaluative exercises in, e.g. Design and Technology (D&T) and science and so have to take proper account of different views.
    Set up debating group to support structuring of argument and structured analysis of opposing arguments.
    Small group work – role-play in realistic goal-setting.
    Exercises to reinforce and develop self-esteem.
    Thinking skill material – curriculum based and free standing – to develop strengths in critical skills and to expose to range of creative skill areas; decision-making material would bring these together.

- Class and school roles which utilise and develop natural organising tendency and skills. Also need to work within different groups but taking specific and agreed role; setting up debating group (including an organisational role) would be good starting point.
    Discussion with mentor on own and other leadership styles as part of development of personal acceptable leadership style.
    Opportunity to devise games linked to other areas of development – e.g. board game to do with 'choice' – and then explain to other participants.
    Extended homework project, possibly linking choice to interest in history curriculum.

- Small group discussion on a range of issues – moral dilemmas, world issues.
    Thinking skill material e.g. on managing community (rewarding importance/contribution to community), famine relief operation.
    Through role-play, appreciating viewpoints and priorities.
    Role-play to understand conflicting and different values.

- Planned and spontaneous opportunities away from class – individual study time both in lessons and after school. Differentiated supported self-study tasks.

> Structured opportunities to work with others on specific tasks – group work – with clearly defined functions within group; chance to discuss usefulness of approach.
>
> Creative opportunities built into structure of range of curricular areas, with tolerance of unconventional responses. Exposure to range of creative material in variety of media.
>
> • Role-play, strengthening own point of view and awareness of other views.
>
> > Thinking skill material/structured role-play in area of decision-making/choice.
> >
> > Give generalisations (e.g. from newspaper, TV) and require judgements on appropriateness/validity.
> >
> > Opportunities for generalising from current affairs, in science, history – and testing with colleagues; debating.

Column one: Differentiating characteristics	Column two: Related needs	Column three: Related suggestions for provision
• An evaluative approach to self and others. High expectations of self and others. Thinks critically; self-critical.		
■ Enjoys organising things – and people – into structure or order; seeks to develop systems, strategies, rules – these may be especially complicated.	■ To be involved in a range of organising opportunities – in different fields, of different types and scale, and with different groups of people.	■ Class and school roles which utilise and develop natural organising tendency and skills. Also need to work within different groups but taking specific and agreed role; setting up
* sometimes comes across as 'bossy' – there have been occasions when other pupils have complained of this	■ To be exposed to problems and tasks which require strategy or system development, or clarity of detail in rules/regulations	debating group (including an organisational role) would be good starting point. Discussion with mentor on own and other leadership styles as part of development of personal acceptable leadership style.
* other children sometimes don't understand complex plans – recent difficulty over invented game when the rest of the group did not understand the rules	■ To explore, practise and develop own leadership style which is valued in school community.	Opportunity to devise games linked to other areas of development – e.g. board game to do with 'choice' – and then explain to other participants. Extended homework project, possibly linking choice to interest in history curriculum.
■ Idealism and strong sense of justice and what is fair; love of truth, equity and fair-play; strong interest in current/world affairs, and matters of great importance.	■ To overcome negative reactions by exploring values to which student is able to be committed.	
* recently upset after seeing TV pictures of famine victims	■ To have access to, and opportunity to explore, current affairs/world events.	Small group discussion on a range of issues – moral dilemmas, world issues. Thinking skill material e.g. on managing community (rewarding importance/
* raised issue of food surplus in Western world		contribution to community), famine relief operation. Through role-play, appreciating viewpoints and priorities. Role-play to understand conflicting and different values.
• Independent, preferring individualised work. Reliant on self.		
• Thinking in alternatives and abstract terms. Sensing and appreciating consequences. Making generalisations, and visualising solutions.		

Figure 2.2 Developing items for column one into the three-column model (in respect of pupil X)

Thoughtfully done, this exercise can be a useful 'shaper' of detailed curriculum provision. Admittedly, it is open to criticism as somewhat simplistic and mechanical. Like all such generalised tools, it is not without a degree of danger.

Nevertheless, I have found it helpful both in terms of groups of children and even the most able in general (i.e. as an INSET (In-Service Education and Training) exercise with a familiarisation emphasis); also (and particularly) in terms of the individual pupil. In this latter context, it is the basis of the Individualised Development Plan (IDP) which I now go on to discuss as one of the features of an appropriately supportive climate for the most able.

Climatic indicators

So, what sort of 'climate' would best suit the developmental requirements, including social and emotional needs, of the most able? What might be legitimately included in a list of 'climatic indicators'? If I were involved in a review or inspection exercise in a school how would I make decisions about the prevailing climate? What evidence would I regard as helpful in forming a view?

Here are suggestions of some key indicators. Their order is not significant, and I acknowledge a degree of overlap between them. I also acknowledge that some of them are difficult areas within which to assemble firm and reliable evidence, and within which to quantify. Also that, even when quantifiable, reliable judgements on their quality might be even more difficult to come by. However, their elusiveness makes them no less desirable or important! It is the qualitative measure with which I am primarily concerned throughout.

I propose seven areas of climatic indicator, as follows: quality of questioning, central importance of metacognitive reflection, emphasis on transfer, involvement of parents in the learning process, problem-solving opportunities, range of available strategies (strategy menu), and provision of individual development programme (IDP).

Each of these is explored in turn.

Quality of questioning

Here I include a whole range of aspects of the questioning process and its quality; in short, the amount, relevance, type, level, range, balance, direction, and spirit of questioning. I use these words deliberately to convey a series of precise concerns and expectations relating to questioning practice.

In terms of amount, I am looking at the pattern of questioning within the lesson. Is the teacher indeed questioning the pupils? Are there in fact opportunities for pupils to formulate and articulate answers, and to evaluate their own and others' responses? Clearly, the questions need to have relevance to the subject in hand, but relevance is perhaps the most obvious of several aspects of question quality; the other quality issues are increasingly more complex.

Much has already been written about the distinction between different types of question; I find the analysis by Kerry (1990) especially useful in that it makes particular reference to a more able context. It is helpful to distinguish between different types of question, and to consider not only whether they are open or closed, but also the extent to which pupil response requires higher cognitive skills rather than simple factual recall. Kerry proposes a hierarchy of nine question types: five are categorised as 'closed' and require 'shorter answers, less thought and little competence in language use by pupils'; four others are categorised as more demanding for able pupils. They are: speculative or hypothesis-generating questions, analytical or reasoning questions, discriminatory questions, and problem-solving questions.

Such consideration of type and level lead to what I see as the centrally important issue of the direction of questioning. In what direction is the questioning taking the pupils' thinking? Do the questions set out to support and develop metacognitive reflection – like, for example those questions and prompts central to the CASE (Cognitive Acceleration through Science Education) project (Adey *et al.* 1989a and b)? Do they support pupils in making links between the work in hand and other areas of work? In other words, are they serving to lead the child one step closer to being able to transfer skills from one context to another? Adey *et al.* (1990) Adey and Shayer (1994) have demonstrated that teachers can develop such directional skills in terms of their focused questioning repertoire.

An important aspect of questioning which relates to issues of type, level and direction alike is that of range and balance. It is important that the most able are exposed to a full range of questions. Again, it is helpful to take Kerry's (1990) list as an illustrative example. Certainly, the most able pupils need ample exposure to questioning within the four more demanding categories detailed above. However, such exposure should not be at the expense of other question types and the lower-order skill development opportunities associated with them. The range and balance of questioning available to the most able would be another indicator of climate appropriateness.

My final suggested consideration of the quality of questioning is the most general and difficult of them all to tie down; it relates to the spirit of the questioning. Part of this relates to the genuineness of the enquiry. For example, does a question which starts: 'What do you think' really mean what it seems to be asking? Is the teacher really interested in the personal view or theory of the pupil? Or is the enquiry actually demanding recall from a previous lesson or the requirement to match with the teacher's line of thought? Additionally, a consideration of the spirit of questioning would include the extent to which the process was enjoyable, and helped to convey a love of enquiry. In short, is it helping to say: 'It's fun to find out – together!'.

Central importance of metacognitive reflection

I have already noted the importance of a deliberately metacognitive direction in relation to questioning.

Metacognition may be simply defined as 'thinking about one's own thinking'. It is argued that central to the development of thinking skills is a corresponding development of metacognitive awareness. As Adey *et al.* (1989b) notes:

> An important part of … developing thinking skills is for pupils to become conscious of and articulate about the sort of thinking they are employing to solve different problems. Thinking back and reflecting aloud helps to develop this consciousness. (p. 5)

Also, that a natural tendency to reflect metacognitively is likely to be more evident, and in evidence earlier, in a more able child. The propensity for metacognitive reflection is a characteristic of high ability that may be developed and enhanced in appropriate climatic conditions.

In considering the extent to which a climate is likely to support and encourage the development of metacognitive reflection, therefore, one would look first and foremost for opportunity. Does the curriculum offer deliberate and structured opportunities for pupils to reflect upon their own thinking processes? Are teachers maximising these opportunities in their curriculum planning and organisation? Are the anticipated outcomes and potential advantages of such reflection shared with, and made clear to, the pupils?

In terms of the last of these questions, the process can be a straightforwardly open one. Consider, for example, the following examples taken from different parts of some material designed to support the development of a range of higher-order thinking skills associated with decision-making (Bentley 1997). Each sets out to encourage reflection on personal thinking processes:

Why did you make this choice?
Try to explain your reasons.
(Imagine that you are talking to a friend who has made a different choice.)

Now list three or four arguments to support YOUR favourite theory.
(Imagine that you have to defend your choice of theory in a class debate.)

Why did you decide on the particular prize that you did?
Are you able to explain the reasoning behind your choice?

The emphasis on metacognition, and shared open reference to it, was reinforced in the project from which these examples are taken by the requirement on the pupils involved to maintain a series of guided diary observations which included these items:

Have you learned anything about the way YOU think?

Can you describe in your own words any thinking processes you used in this Unit?

Emphasis on transfer

Closely linked with metacognition is the notion of transfer. Transfer, or bridging, is the process of lifting or adapting skills and competencies learned in one context and applying them in another. It is strikingly illustrated in relation to the CASE project where groups of children exposed to the project's emphasis on cognitive reflection and analysis in their learning in science performed significantly better in examinations taken either two or three years later (Adey and Shayer 1994). In doing so, they demonstrated that learning strategies had been internalised. The fact that these same experimental group pupils also performed better in some subject areas other than science illustrates another and central aspect of transfer: that of the transfer of skills and strategies from one curriculum area to another.

You will gather from this that transfer is a more complex process than perhaps suggested by my earlier simplistic definition. It is not appropriate here to pursue this topic in detail, but it is worth just noting the important distinction between 'near' transfer (where there is an obvious similarity between the original learning experience and the new situation) and 'far' transfer (where there is a clear difference between them). Further distinctions are drawn between 'specific' and 'non-specific' transfer, and between 'deep' and 'surface' transfer structures. Detterman (1993) reinforces the very important point that 'it is far transfer of deep structure that most researchers would characterise as typical of highly intelligent behaviour ... It is also far transfer of deep structure that is most difficult to get' (p. 5).

Its complexity is a factor in making transfer a process which is difficult to assess outside a rigorous experimental model. However, it is possible to take a very practical and every-day view of the transfer process, and to routinely focus children's attention on it as part of metacognitive emphasis and as part of the sharing (with the pupil) of intended learning outcomes. I set out to do this at a very basic but practical level in the thinking skill work units to which I have already made mention. In their Unit Diaries, the pupils were asked:

In doing this Unit, have you worked on any skills which you think might be useful in other problem-solving situations? If so, ... which skills? ... which situations?

Parents were also asked to look out for examples of transfer in supporting their child through discussion. It was a Parent Supporter's Diary which offered one of the more striking examples of transfer. This was in connection with units which had required the student to approach some issues and tasks from another person's standpoint; to see and appreciate other points of view:

> *Have you noticed any evidence of … the student using something you think was a [Unit] skill transferred to another situation?*
> *Having asked questions about the Maastricht Treaty, Paul was trying to consider the French and English points of view.*

It is possible, then, to teach for transfer and to enhance the natural propensity of the able child to engage in transfer. Key to this is the teacher's awareness of the potential of, and need for, transfer, and the provision of opportunities to enable transfer to take place and to be recognised. The real skill of the teacher is in prompting transfer links – and in knowing when, and to what extent, to intervene in this respect. The quality and timing of intervention is crucial. No intervention might well mean that 'bridges' remain unbuilt. Too much intervention will prevent the pupil from being the bridge builder, and so taking maximum advantage from the opportunity. It is knowing just when (and when not) to nudge the transfer process, and how hard to nudge it!

As already mentioned, this teaching skill, in providing and supporting transfer opportunities, and so nurturing and enhancing the development of natural transfer strategies, is neither an easy one to achieve nor to measure. It is, however, a significant feature of a climate conducive to the development of social and emotional needs in the most able child.

Involvement of parents in the learning process

In the preceding sections, exploring issues of both metacognition and transfer, I mentioned observations made by parents in structured 'diary' entries linked to a thinking skill programme for able pupils. This serves as a practical example of a developed role for parents in the learning process; also, of a specific opportunity for supporting the needs of the most able in an independent study situation.

The quality of parental responses and general involvement varied. When it worked well, the quality and detail of observation was considerable; for example:

> Jane still repeats that her 'weakness' lies in her use and range of information, and that her 'strength' lies in the analysis of information, computation of data and this type of task.

> Anne was previously 'over-concerned' about being 'right' or 'wrong'. She feels that she has developed skills and confidence in this regard.

Certainly, the overall picture provided sufficiently encouraging pointers to the potential value of developing the parental role alongside a range of school-based involvement.

There have, of course, been large-scale projects which have relied upon, and shaped, a supportive parental role; the best known is the IMPACT mathematics material (Mertens and Leather 1993). There are also many individual schools where valuable fine-tuning of the parental role continues to take place. In too many schools, however, there has been little development of a remote parental involvement within a traditional homework expectation; partnership potential, particularly in terms of the most able pupils, remains largely untapped.

Recent guidance in respect of homework has seen both DfEE (1998a) and OFSTED (Weston 1999) stress the importance for schools of building a partnership with parents. This would be characterised by teachers 'collaborating closely with parents on home-based learning, explaining aims and methods and showing them how to help their children'. Workshops and other support provided by the school would increase parents' confidence in developing their more active role. There has been further opportunity through projects related to the DfEE's (1998b) 'Extending Opportunities' initiative. In one pilot which I have monitored, involving two 9–13 middle schools working with a museum of historical buildings, parental involvement and commitment has been emphasised. Initiatives like this encourage an overlapping of the parental role into areas of more conventional curriculum development. Opportunities in relation to the most able, in respect of whom differentiated homework provision is a neglected aspect of overall differentiation strategy, are of particular significance. Evidence of the genuine parental involvement and utilisation in the broad extended learning context, and the associated innovative use of 'homework' as a means of differentiating and extending curricular experiences, is a key indicator of a climate supportive of the particular needs of the most able.

Problem-solving opportunities

In earlier discussion of question quality, I mentioned the notion of open-endedness. I have a colleague who talks in the same way, and also very helpfully, of open-ceilingedness – that is, not creating a limit on the child's thinking. It is interesting to apply these related concepts to the issue of problem-solving.

Its inclusion in this list shows that I see problem-solving as a key climatic indicator. It is an important part of the overall process of providing opportunities for metacognitive reflection and transfer. It could additionally be an aspect of differentiated provision for the most able. A problem-solving based project might also serve to support other climatic indicators in that it could have a significant out-of-school component, could set out to enlist parental and other external support, and could last over a period of time; it could also be linked to a range of curricular areas or be cross-curricular in nature.

Back to this notion of open-endedness; it would, of course, be possible to present problems which are seen to be helpful in developing a range of skills (like strategy formation, for example) yet which are closed in that they lead to a right or accepted answer and/or route to their solution. I want to make the crude distinction between these and problems which have no accepted answer or solution route. Then to impress the importance of the latter, while acknowledging the need for balance between the two broad types. I can best illustrate the potential value in this context of the open-ended problem by giving you an example. It is based (as are many of the problems I use) upon a newspaper article (Keys 1990) which reported the discovery, in a Cheddar cave, of a prehistoric animal bone – actually the tibia of an arctic hare. This bone was distinguished by a series of notches – in groups of 28, 29 and 29 or 30 – cut into it along one edge. Pupils are asked to suggest why Stone Age man, living in caves under the Somerset hills, might have cut the notches in this bone.

I have used this activity more than once with groups of very able pupils. It reinforces the very important principle of personal opinion being valued. Pupils grapple with the idea that there is no 'right' answer (though we later explore some 'expert' theories) and that I genuinely mean it when I ask 'What do *you* think?'

Look at the following responses from one pupil to the simple question about the bone and its notches. Consider first the richness of thinking, and then the potential contribution of the exercise to metacognitive reflection:

> It might have been a kind of register for a meeting held every so often.
> They could be part of a game equivalent to bingo nowadays.
> The marks might be showing what each man has caught while hunting.
> They might just have been made by accident, perhaps it's where they cut the meat everyday, and the knife goes through.
>
> … some children enjoy closed questions and I've realised that I'm one of those children. But I find it difficult when posed with an open question. I have trouble thinking of unrealistic things. I usually tend to write down things that might well happen.

And all this from something as 'ordinary' as a newspaper article. No expensive or complex resources involved. Just the right question, opportunity and climate.

The example I have used as an open-ended – and 'open-ceilinged' – problem raises and additionally exemplifies two further issues. Qualities which very able children welcome in relation to presented problems, and which may be seen to be supportive in terms of a range of their needs, are reality of context and social emphasis. This is a real bone found in a real cave; the notches were made by real people.

A better example of the social and 'real world' emphases concerns a piece of role-play centred problem solving. Groups of able pupils were given detailed briefing notes on an African famine relief operation, and then a specific role within which they were required to develop bids for project funding and also justify their project's requirements and prioritisation. The role-play was another critical factor in meeting a social need which is experience in evaluating, appreciating and acknowledging other points of view. There is a natural tendency towards egocentricity, and an ability to be fiercely critical of other viewpoints. The situation is the more difficult when other points of view – from other able pupils – are equally well structured, presented and fought for!

An activity at a thinking skill workshop (for able pupils in Years Six to Eight) admirably demonstrates a reluctance to concede a firmly held stance. It was linked to the notched bone exercise, but could be replicated in a range of contexts. I asked each of the students to choose, from their own creative and sometimes lengthy list of alternatives, their personal favourite explanation for the incisions; also, to make notes justifying their choice. Participants were then put into groups of three (with me ensuring that all three had different 'favourites') and asked to present and justify their choice to the other two who, in turn, could question and offer critical comment. Each group then had to agree on one of the three favourites to take forward as 'group favourite'. In several of the groups, the participants found it impossible to reach agreement!

Range of available strategies (strategy menu)

The point has already been made in my introductory comments that it is impossible to identify one single strategy as being *the* ideal form of provision. I know, too, that examples of provision within the complex area of extension and enrichment are being addressed in detail elsewhere in this book; I shall not duplicate that detailed consideration.

At present, there is great interest in acceleration and 'fast-tracking'. It is first important to acknowledge that acceleration may take a range of forms: at its most extreme, it will involve placement in another year group, typically one or even two years ahead of the year group to which the pupil is chronologically matched, for all curricular and extracurricular activity; it may involve advancement in a particular curriculum area through taking all lessons in the subject in question in another year group or even another school; or it may involve a softer version still, where acceleration in an individual subject area involves exposure to a more advanced curriculum, but experienced through individual programming within the chronologically appropriate age group – perhaps with some visits to another class built in to the arrangement.

I have also seen what has been described as accelerated provision in a range of cross-curricular and even extra-curricular activities: working on advanced skills in Information and Communication Technology; participation in weekend workshop activities with groups of older pupils; involvement with an older year group in a programme to support the development of thinking skills. However, while these may be seen as variations of acceleration, they may also be legitimately viewed as enrichment strategies for students based in their chronologically appropriate year group. The distinction becomes blurred.

Let us return to the acceleration models involving regular placement with older pupils. It needs to be acknowledged that whereas there may well be real or perceived advantages in transfer to another age group for all or part of the curriculum, there may also be attendant disadvantages. They may simply be organisational; perhaps resulting from a mismatch of timetable in different year groups or mismatch of lesson times in different schools. They may be curricular; for example, in terms of missed experience or understanding (the significance of which may well not manifest itself until later). They may be social and/or emotional; for example, concerning the acceptance of a less socially (and perhaps also less physically) mature pupil by an older age group, or the potentially damaging effects on a current friendship group. Social and emotional factors need to be properly taken into account by all the parties involved in the discussion on possible accelerated provision before a decision is taken. It may well be the case that a mentoring arrangement needs to be put into place to support particular social and emotional needs identified in relation to the acceleration.

Of course, in a basic provision model enrichment is often represented as the alternative to acceleration. Simplistically, it may be seen as involving a range of strategies designed to broaden or deepen curricular experiences normally associated with the year group in question. It is based on a sideways rather than an upward emphasis. It might involve, as has already been noted, qualitatively different ICT experiences to support the curriculum (through, for example, the Internet or through access to other 'expert' input); masterclasses; summer schools and other workshops (subject-based or cross-curricular); differentiated homework opportunities, possibly longer-term and involving research); individualised school-based projects (again, some longer-term); supported self-study opportunity (with the appropriate level of support); or small group working (with other able pupils). The range of enrichment possibilities, combinations and variations of possibilities, is endless. It may even involve exposure to subjects which are not part of the standard curriculum; studying, say, astronomy as an additional subject is presumably not acceleration, though taking GCSE in it earlier than Year 11 might be!

It is unhelpful to view accelerated provision and enriched provision as alternatives. Placement of a pupil in another year group, following thorough discussion embracing all those involved and agreement on an overall plan of action, is not in itself the answer. Working in the chronologically advanced year group may not present significantly qualitatively different challenges for the accelerated pupil, nor the stimulation of a significantly more mature peer group. It can, therefore, be disappointing if not supported by a range of enrichment strategies.

This form of acceleration needs to be supported by a whole range of enrichment strategies to make it properly effective. And if this form of acceleration is not seen as the best option – perhaps because of social or emotional considerations – an individualised programme of enriched provision may well include some element of differentiated acceleration, perhaps for a subject, club, workshop, or supported self-study course.

A menu of genuinely flexible provision, with a genuine will to find individually matched and planned routes through the full range of options available, is vital for the needs of the most able child. Built into this route-finding must be proper consideration of social and emotional, as well as academic, needs. Route-finding leads me to the last of my seven climatic indicators.

Provision of individual development programme (IDP)

I have already largely dealt with this aspect of planning and provision earlier (in considering the three column link-strengthening exercise) and so shall not repeat that process and its importance. This is not to diminish its significance. The willingness of a school to prepare and review regularly an individualised programme for a very able pupil, and its commitment in terms of time and energy, is a key indicator of climate appropriateness.

In some schools this plan is referred to as an Individual(ised) Education Plan (or Programme) (IEP), and includes a number of the features normally associated with the sort of IEP with which colleagues working with statemented pupils are familiar. The emphasis of the more able version of such a document should be on curriculum adaptation and development, and the plan might legitimately involve a whole range of longer and shorter-term strategies. Comments on the plan will serve as an additional detailed record to supplement other routine recording of each child's school progress.

I admit a personal preference for the use of the term Individual(ised) Development Programme (Plan) (IDP). This is not mere semantics! It is in part to separate the documentation from the legislatively-based IEP and the resourcing which might be expected to accompany it. There are significant differences in the way the contents of such a plan/programme may be balanced and shaped in relation to the most able. More importantly, my terminology preference relates mainly to the advantage that the emphasis on 'Development' allows for proper acknowledgement of the social and emotional aspects of such a plan. It does not emphasise the narrowly curricular, but would enable (and perhaps even encourage) considerations like, for example, experience of team-membership, role-play, or acknowledgement of the viewpoints of other pupils, to be included; also, where relevant, additionally to shape curriculum content, organisation and presentation.

One final point relating to the importance of the IEP/IDP is the need for it genuinely to be a document which is shared between school and home at all stages of its development and review. In this way, it supports the proper scale and level of parental involvement in curriculum planning and provision.

Flexibility

There is a common thread running through the climatic indicators which I have outlined. It is that of flexibility. The school which is effective in meeting the needs of the most able is not simply reflecting characteristics and provision described. It also has developed the ability, and the confidence, to be flexible in terms of any one, or any combination, of the indicators.

This flexibility will, as already noted, be likely to be effectively demonstrated in the quality of an Individualised Development Programme (IDP). This will reflect the school's ability to put together, by adopting a 'pick and mix' approach, a personalised package of support. Essentially, to construct a programme for the individual pupil. The system here sets out to be flexible, regarding flexibility is its basis, its rationale, rather than being a quality towards which it is forced (perhaps through the application of external pressure).

To illustrate flexibility in action, I have listed some of the 'headlines' of provision packages assembled to support two very able pupils. In each case, I prefix the key aspects of planned provision with a very brief (and inadequate) summary of the pupil's background.

Both cases, though fictionalised, are based upon work currently or recently in hand with pupils of high academic ability. Also, each is based upon thoughtful consideration of the characteristics and learning style of the pupil involved, and upon analysis of the learning support needs.

In the 'headline' sections I have included only some of the individual provision; I have not included more basic strategies. Assume, for example, that for each there are additional opportunities: for individualised work during the school day; for the advantages of setting/group working as and when appropriate; and for exposure to a range of differentiation strategies within the classroom. This is not, of course, to understate the importance and potential significance of such common-place aspects of provision. However, the intention is to give a flavour of an individualised programme, and at the same time to demonstrate the very real relevance of the climatic indicators in shaping it.

Adam

Chronologically Year Four, but working as if Year Five. General high ability, though some insecurity in mathematics seemingly resulting from unhappy early experiences in the subject. Decision agreed to accelerate him by one year within the three-tier system so that he started middle school (9–13) a year early (i.e. end of Year Three to beginning of Year Five). General agreement that Adam would benefit from being part of the working community and ethos of a larger school with older pupils. During discussions prior to transfer, concerns about the social aspects of the move were raised; however, there were already some difficulties of frustration with peer group, and difficulties in forming and sustaining friendships with peers. Adam cited lack of common interests as a significant factor in this.

'**Headlines**' from Adam's enriched IDP provision include:
- linked electronically, through LEA, with group of similarly exceptionally able pupils to exchange e-mail and work on LEA-generated problem-solving material;
- involved in problem-solving masterclass (LEA Intranet);
- science teacher from high school takes lesson with Adam's class twice a half-term; also, works with small group of very able pupils, including Adam, on science enrichment topics;
- individualised homework projects;
- unlimited use of school IT facilities at lunchtime and after school (with teacher support available as required);
- staff mentor appointed to support development of Adam's study skills and his personal organisation of schoolwork/homework; and
- with able pupils in other year groups in his school, participation in a one-day thinking skills workshop on decision-making.

Lucy

Year Eight student in her final year of a 9–13 middle school in three-tier system. There had been discussion about jumping a year group on more than one occasion; a full review of this possibility was held during the first year at middle school, with the possibility in mind of jumping to the third middle school year (i.e. end of Year Five to beginning of Year Seven). The decision, to which Lucy's parents and Lucy herself were party, was against taking this step. An area of particular concern related to Lucy's general lack of confidence and lack of belief in aspects of her own high ability. Coupled with this, the extent to which she and a small group of friends worked well cooperatively and relied upon the mutual support within the group. It was agreed that Lucy, who was in the younger half of the year group, might well find it difficult to adjust socially and emotionally to year group transfer.

'Headlines' from Lucy's enriched IDP provision include:

- programme of thinking skill support, designed to enhance development of range of skills associated with confidence in forming and justifying own views, and thinking creatively; programme organised and monitored by the school, but completed largely at home and with parental involvement as required (variation of supported self-study);
- differentiated homework programme (which acknowledges both weight of additional thinking skills project and need for suitably challenging tasks);
- attendance at DfEE funded 10 day Arts Summer School run through local high school but involving work with both professional artist and writer and assignments at art gallery;
- linked to mentor who is able sixth-former at high school, with weekly meeting for structured discussion;
- part of a group of able students from different middle schools in LEA-organised residential 'thinking workshop';
- with other members of a group of able pupils in her year group, regular access via computer link with similarly able group in a Texas school; academic and social agenda;
- membership of school public speaking team (which engages in friendly competition with a small number of other schools in the area); and
- a school-monitored arrangement: a university science student shares, by post, individual issues/insights associated with her own research project; Paula's views are actively sought, with ideas on her research exchanged.

General applicability

I noted in my introductory comments that those opportunities outlined as desirable in respect of the most able do, in fact, apply in the broadest sense to all children. There is a sense in which we are doing no more than describing high quality, thoughtful teaching, coupled with the provision of relevant and appropriately challenging opportunities.

At the same time, I would argue that there are some issues of good teaching and management, and the consequent provision of appropriate learning opportunities, which have particular relevance to the most able. I have drawn attention to these – including, for example, issues associated with a natural tendency to transfer, to engage in metacognitive reflection, to seek out opportunities for individual study, and to respond to higher-order questioning.

The way forward: a 'climate audit'

What of the way forward? Quality provision for the most able is a product of its planning and preparation. It can be achieved only with due consideration of carefully analysed need. And it can be achieved only within an appropriate and conducive climate.

It is important that all those involved in this providing process, in whatever capacity, continue to monitor and evaluate carefully, and to use their findings to influence decision-making and to shape future provision. In the spirit of greater emphasis on self-review and self-evaluation, I end with a list of questions reflecting the climatic conditions I have proposed.

SELF-REVIEW QUESTIONS

Ten questions to support school self-review.
1. *A question relating to each indicator/climate area*:
   ✔ Is there an appropriate range and balance of questioning, including sufficient open and higher-order questioning, for the most able?
   ✔ Are there structured opportunities, in all areas of the curriculum, for pupils to engage in metacognitive reflection as part of (support for) the development of thinking skills?
   ✔ Are pupils encouraged, through the provision of appropriate support and opportunity, to both transfer skills and to reflect on the transfer process and its significance?
   ✔ Are opportunities created for parental involvement in the learning process, and is there extended opportunity for learning outside the school day, including provision of differentiated homework?
   ✔ Is there a range of problem-solving opportunities across the curriculum, including sufficient open-ended and 'open-ceilinged' problems with social and other 'real' contexts?
   ✔ Is a full range of organisational strategies available and utilised, including both enrichment-emphasising strategies and those involving accelerated provision?
   ✔ Is there opportunity for an individualised development programme (IDP) of adapted curricular and other provision, clearly based on need analysis and making reference to social and emotional as well as academic development, to be constructed and monitored?
2. *Three questions which may be applied to each of the seven indicators/climate areas in turn*:

> ✔ Is there sufficient staff awareness of, and feel for, the needs of the most able in relation to this aspect of climate?
> ✔ Are there training or other professional development needs in terms of this climate area?
> ✔ How is this aspect of the climate monitored and evaluated; how does this evaluation in turn influence future decision-making?

Although these are worded as if from the standpoint of a school manager, adviser or inspector, they can easily be adapted to reflect the role of class teacher, parent, governor or any other partner in the learning process. They can apply to a school of any age-grouping, and to any class within it. Each can usefully be supported with additional questions in the same area. Each can be made tougher by supplementing it with: How? To what extent? In what ways? What are the gaps?

Above all, the self-review should be a positive exercise! The greater emphasis on the needs of the most able, the significance of thinking skills in supporting curricular provision, and the advantages of self-evaluation combine to create an opportunity to move things forward. We should take it.

References

Adey, P. and Shayer, M. (1994) *Really Raising Standards: Cognitive Integration and Academic Achievement.* London: Routledge.

Adey, P., Shayer, M. and Yeates, C. (1989a) *Thinking Science: The Curriculum Materials of the Cognitive Acceleration through Science Education (CASE) Project.* London: Macmillan.

Adey, P., Shayer, M. and Yeates, C. (1989b) *Thinking Science: The Curriculum Materials of the Cognitive Acceleration through Science Education (CASE) Project. Teacher's Guide.* London: Macmillan.

Adey, P., Shayer, M. and Yeates, C. (1990) *Better Learning: A Report from the Cognitive Acceleration through Science Education (CASE) Project.* London: Centre for Educational Studies, Kings College, University of London.

Bentley, R. (1997) *The Development of Distance Learning Material to Support Decision-Related Thinking Skills in More Able Children* (unpublished PhD thesis, University of Southampton).

Clark, B. (1988) *Growing Up Gifted,* 3rd edn. Columbus, OH: Merrill.

Clark, C. and Callow, R. (1998) *Educating Able Children: Resource Issues and Processes for Teachers.* London: David Fulton Publishers.

Detterman, D. K. and Sternberg, R. J. (1993) 'The case for the prosecution: transfer as an epiphenomenon', in Detterman, D. K. and Sternberg, R. J. *Transfer on Trial: Intelligence, Cognition and Instruction.* Norwood, NJ: Ablex Publishing Corporation.

DfEE (1998a) *Homework: Guidelines for Primary and Secondary Schools.* London: DfEE Publications.

DfEE (1998b) *Extending Opportunity: A National Framework for Study Support.* London: DfEE Publications.

Eyre, D. (1997) *Able Children in Ordinary Schools.* London: David Fulton Publishers.

George, D. (1997) *The Challenge of the Able Child,* 2nd edn. London: David Fulton Publishers.

Kerry, T. (1990) *Teaching Bright Pupils in Mixed Ability Classes.* London: Macmillan.

Keys, D. (1990) 'Notched bones may be cannibals' calendars', *The Independent,* 14 April 1990.

Leyden, S. (1998) *Supporting the Child of Exceptional Ability,* 2nd edn. London: David Fulton Publishers.

Mertens, R. and Leather, R. (1993) *IMPACT Project Material.* Leamington Spa: Scholastic Publications Ltd.

Weston, P. (1999) *Homework: Learning From Practice.* London: The Stationery Office.

CHAPTER 3

Extension and enrichment programmes: 'A place I could fit in'

Julian Whybra

In discussing the suitability of extension and enrichment programmes as appropriate and desirable provision for gifted and talented children there are four areas to explore:

- the rationale behind such programmes;
- the wider implications of creating intellectual peer communities and of providing a high level of resource as integral aspects of meeting the needs of the gifted and talented;
- the strategies in organisation and methods which may be manipulated to allow greater opportunities for gifted children to work at appropriate levels; and
- the basic underlying principles which should govern the teacher's preparation of work for gifted children.

A rationale

The major needs of gifted and talented children are: firstly, recognition of their ability; and secondly, an understanding of, and an effective response to, their emotional, social and intellectual needs.

Socially, gifted children, like all other children, need to belong to a group and within it, to play, to give and take, and to be accepted. They need contact with peers, a consequent understanding of others' as well as their own needs, and experience of living in the community. They need to develop fully as individuals but they must also recognise that exercising their individuality brings obligations and the respect of others' rights. Furthermore, society requires their vital contribution as adults; an isolated, lonely, unsocialised gifted adult not only experiences deep personal frustration and unhappiness but society is deprived and impoverished by the absence of any contribution from her/him.

It has been repeatedly noted that intellectually gifted children have a developmental discontinuity in relation to their chronological peers and it is now widely recognised that emotional development, and even morality, are more closely correlated with mental rather than chronological age. It is, of course, essential that gifted children have balanced, healthy emotional development if they are to develop into rounded, mature adults. Emotionally and socially, a gifted child who has the same mental age as older children will resemble older intellectual peers much more than chronological peers (Gross 1994). The contact, then, for emotional development should be with intellectual peers. As Foster (1986) points out, the disparity between gifted youngsters' experience of the world and that of their chronological peers, can often lead, initially, to a sense of difference and then to feelings of loneliness and isolation.

Extension and enrichment programmes, in congregating gifted children, can alleviate or prevent this emotional isolation by creating true 'peer' groups of students who are at the same developmental stage, socially, emotionally and intellectually (Rogers 1991). In addition to considering social and emotional development, one must also be aware that gifted children have specific intellectual needs different from those of normal children. In order to feel normal in a learning situation they need some contact with intellectual peers for the experiences of exchanging ideas, mental stimulation and the sharing of interests. They need rapid movement through basic stages to depth. They have exceptional abilities and skills that require development: the ability to grasp a concept quickly; to absorb information rapidly, both in depth and breadth; to reason abstractly; to see unusual relationships; to make conceptual leaps; to solve problems; to relate information; and to anticipate consequences and outcomes. They need to be challenged to the point of failure and to experience the satisfaction of intellectual exercise. The reality is that many gifted children are reluctant to face failure; they are too used to easy, instant success and with a very little effort they are able to satisfy the teacher's demands and thereby fail to develop work habits requiring self-discipline and perseverance.

As well as participating in group activities, they need to develop their own specific interests with opportunities for contact with experts in specialist fields. They need to experience the satisfaction of rapidly developing ideas, the interrogation of another's expertise, and the sheer pleasure of discussing and developing an argument with an intellectual equal or superior.

Consider the following selection of relevant quotations from a survey of students (and their parents), who attended GIFT Curriculum Extension Courses (Whybra 1998):

The experience of a different approach from that of a school with peers who respond quickly to ideas is invaluable. The opportunity to study a topic in depth for several hours and at a consistently high level is a new experience, as is often the subject matter itself.

The difference from learning at school is that the whole approach can be and is more adult. The pupils are more able to explore ideas, go off at a tangent and spend time developing their thoughts and perceptions.

It is the challenge that makes the greatest lasting difference, even for the less outgoing student who can feel isolated in the mainstream school set-up. It is the fact that during the course it is not exceptional to be intelligent – it is the norm.

My son went to flex his mental muscles away from the rigidity of the National Curriculum, to meet and make new friends with other gifted children and adults, to be able to relax and not feel he stands out so much, and to get some practice with organising himself in the practical aspects of a residential course. It met all our expectations – he always comes back happy, excited by what he has done, relaxed, and noticeably more confident.

I wanted to meet other people who understood what I was saying. I wanted the opportunity to be myself. I can't thank GIFT enough for everything.

It is common for both gifted child and parents to require guidance and perhaps counselling. The child too often sees her/his gift not as a blessing but as a curse. Gifted students need reassurance that they are normal yet different and need the chance to discuss a problem with a sensitive listener who will empathise and offer constructive help and advice.

Wider implications

The specific needs of the gifted child in school are closely interwoven and interdependent with those of the teacher. Apart from having an awareness of, and a sympathy with, the gifted child's problems, the teacher will have to be sufficiently emotionally mature to accept a child with a high potential (as well as sometimes a greater ability than the teacher her/himself), such that there is acceptance of the role of being a learner with the child, an acceptance of dealing in new and unfamiliar territory.

The teacher also needs to understand the learning patterns of gifted children, to be able to recognise the qualitative differences in children's responses and their levels of conceptualisation so that s/he can plan and guide the children's learning programme accordingly.

Current educational philosophy and practice militate against this approach. As the teacher's role widened and developed in the 1990s, pressure has constantly increased. School organisation and school or LEA ethos can inhibit the teacher's efforts by diminishing opportunities for creative, innovative, flexible activities and work programmes. The Department for Education and Employment's imposition of a systematised framework from above (as in its Education Action Zones, Excellence in Cities, and Gifted and Talented initiatives) limits the school's room to manoeuvre in terms of individual approach and policy.

The average class of 30 students with the whole gamut of physical, social, mental, emotional, and intellectual characteristics requires a teacher with outstanding stamina, patience and talents if all the students' needs are to be met. Various degrees of streaming or setting may reduce the range of abilities in the class, but even in such situations the gifted child is still outstanding and the range of abilities considerable. Even a teacher skilled in practising class differentiation can find that classroom discipline, organisation and management prevent the effective assumption of the advisory role as senior co-learner which working with gifted children so often requires. Classroom differentiation alone is not an educational panacea that will, at a stroke, create systematic tidiness in the delivery of the National Curriculum and solve the problem of providing effective provision to the top end of the ability range. Even effective differentiation is, by itself, an insufficient response to the needs of such children. The difficulty of a gifted child responding to the teacher's stimulus or challenge in the classroom must not be underestimated. Anti-academic peer-group pressure, inside and outside class, may be considerable and sticking one's head over the intellectual parapet is a dangerous occupation for a child.

Peer-group pressure is the single most important factor governing a child's academic success at school (Winiarski-Jones 1988). In comparing IQs with exam results, it has been found that most able students fall into one of four groups: the academics, who work hard and do well; the attention-seekers, who are insecure, vie for the teacher's attention, and do less well; the fun-seekers, who, bored or frustrated, do little work but are expert last-minute revisers and thereby underachieve slightly; and the anti-authority group, who reject education and do badly. Bright children are under immense pressure to conform to the latter, becoming gradually more and more inwardly angry with themselves and unhappy. The tyranny of the peer group can clearly hold back many teenagers from academic success. Taken to extremes such unhappiness can turn into depression. The growing problem of suicide among intellectually gifted children has been the focus of research among American psychologists working with the gifted (Webb *et al.* 1983). It has also recently been the subject matter of headlines in British newspapers (with particular references to instances of bullying, anti-academic peer-group pressure and Asperger Syndrome).

Examine the depth of feeling contained in these replies to a survey from children who attended Essex LEA extension and enrichment courses (Whybra 1989):

> I have discovered a lot about myself during the last four days… at last, I don't feel that I am some kind of exceptional freak. Other people have the same problems as I do; being ostracised by classmates seems to be a common problem amongst us, and attempting to be 'one of the crowd' by speaking the same way as others seems a common remedy.

> Before I came on this course, I thought I was out on my own. By this, I mean that I would never find a person who could communicate with me. Now I find that a lot of worry and depression has been lifted off my mind and consequently I have changed. Before I never quite believed in myself or my eventual purpose in life; now I do.

> I am a very deep thinker and spend hours pondering over various books on philosophy, sociology and world religions. I have not yet met anyone who thinks along the same lines as I do, although I came nearer to it on this course than previously. I spend far too much time daydreaming, creating whole new worlds and getting totally lost trying to figure out why, what and when, where and how. As a rule I find I cannot get on with people of my own age … I sometimes feel a bit of a social outcast … an outsider.

It must also be stated that an appropriate provision of resources in the school is an essential requirement for effective provision. The reality is sadly that all too often resources are limited, particularly for gifted children who simply increase the nature of the problem by racing through books, projects, materials during their first week in school (and generally before the teacher has had a chance to look at them). Certainly the gifted child will learn something in school, but most gifted students work significantly below their true ability. There are many studies (Whitmore 1980, Gross 1993) indicating the nature and size of this problem and it can be argued that probably over 50 per cent of gifted students work, in school, four or five years below their abilities. An early study (Hollingworth 1942) claimed that children of IQ 140 waste half their time in the classroom, while children of IQ 180 waste all their time. Recent research on highly gifted students suggests that this is no exaggeration (Gross 1993). In recognition of this problem the Department for Education and Employment's 1999 remit for its Advisory Group on Gifted and Talented Children refers to ensuring that 'throughout their education [gifted and talented children] receive the teaching and ongoing support they need to achieve the maximum of which they are capable; and all schools sustain a culture which celebrates excellence and rewards high achievement' (p. 5).

In 1989 in a study of 200 20 to 26 year olds, who as children of 14 to 15 had participated in Essex LEA's Curriculum Extension Project between 1978 and 1983, 98 per cent described their attendance as the single greatest determining factor in the success of their subsequent school academic careers. Furthermore, 152 of them had engaged, were engaged or were intending to engage in post-graduate, higher-degree research. Here are some more responses to the 1998 survey of former GIFT Curriculum Extension Course participants:

> [The courses] changed the way I looked at learning completely. I'm about to begin a research M.Phil. at Cambridge and I don't think I'd have ever been this enthusiastic without having experience of research type work at such an early age.

> GIFT made a lasting difference in many ways. It taught me many of the study skills I am utilising in work, for my degree and life in general. I have much more confidence, am more outgoing, and much happier.

> I will always have memories of the courses. They have kept me learning and wanting to learn. These things will carry on so they have made a difference.

School-based or specialist off-site day/residential extension and enrichment courses provide a setting where heterogeneity can establish itself; where safety-in-numbers can combat anti-academic peer-group pressure; where gifted children are automatically accepted and can cultivate social skills; where they can have contact with intellectual (but not necessarily chronological) peers, learn to understand others' needs and opinions and find a sounding board for their own; where they can experience the joy of academic success but fail 'safely' if need be; and where they can develop their talents at their own natural pace and be allowed to fulfil their potential.

Students with specific talents in athletics, sport, music and drama have always met in the past, out of school, for intensive work with their talented peers. Congregation of academically-talented students is a response, along the same lines, to the acceptance that students with specific talents need the opportunity to work together for some period for optimisation of their potential.

Placing gifted children, with some frequency and with some expectation of continuity, in a small group of other congregated students who have the same levels of ability, reasoning capacity, and interests as themselves, offers reassurance that there are others like themselves, and that they are not 'weird'. Far from inducing conceit, the companionship of kindred spirits may show the exceptionally able student, sometimes for the first time, that there are others as able, or more able, and that s/he can learn from them. Virtually every educator and psychologist of note working in gifted education advocates that for self-optimisation of their intellectual potential and the development of a healthy realistic self-image, intellectually-gifted students should be homogeneously grouped for at least part of the time. (Stanley 1979, Wallace 1981, Tannenbaum 1983, Webb *et al.* 1983, Feldhusen 1985, Rogers 1991, Wallace and Adams 1993, Benbow and Lubinski 1996, Renzulli and Purcell 1996 and VanTassel-Baska 1998). There are various ways in which this can be done.

Strategies in school organisation and methods

Cluster grouping involves congregating students from a number of neighbourhood schools at a central location for regular short-term enrichment courses. Schools share staffing, material resources and any costs involved. For example, the Hertford Schools' Able Pupil Consortium (Townsend, Goff's, and Richard Hale Schools) rotates location of the venue among consortium schools and buys in outside expertise to deliver enrichment courses. Staff are released to attend with students on an in-service training basis. The Harlow Schools' Able Child Consortium (Stewards, Burnt Mill, Passmores, St. Mark's, Mark Hall, and Brays Grove Schools) runs a similar scheme but additionally uses consortium schools' staff as course lecturers. Frequency and continuity allow for the formation of social relationships and individual friendships outside the course. The Braintree Schools' Able Child Consortium (Tabor, Alec Hunter, and Notley Schools) has gone one step further by staffing its enrichment course entirely internally while using outside expertise to organise and run residential weekend courses. Bexley LEA, however, employs solely outside expertise to run a programme of Saturday masterclasses and residential courses for (and at no cost to) children within the borough.

Schools have also created in-school cluster groupings within Year Groups. For example, one Essex school where eight mathematically gifted students in Year Six have been placed in an otherwise heterogeneous class with a teacher whose particular interest and area of competence is mathematics. This particular teacher is prepared to differentiate the class's mathematics syllabus to cater for these children's particular talents and there are enough of them to warrant the time and effort involved in creating a differentiated programme of study. The result has been that the children encourage and assist each other in individual and group projects, engage in self-learning independently of the teacher, and literally run the programme by themselves.

There has been an upsurge in the number of schools establishing withdrawal programmes and, after-classroom differentiation, this is the strategy most frequently used to cater for the exceptionally able. Students are withdrawn from their usual classes (either on a fixed-timetable, or rotational basis) to work together for a set or variable period per week on enrichment and extension work. Such a scheme has the advantage of enabling students for a few hours per week to meet with others of similar abilities and interests in a small group setting. Students who have found it necessary to under-achieve for reasons of peer acceptance, discover a set of peers who esteem, rather than denigrate, the pursuit of excellence. In addition, the specialist lecturer, when s/he is aware of the special needs and learning styles of the exceptionally able, is able to offer, because of the extreme heterogeneity of the student group, materials and methods suitable to its level and styles of learning and to foster more abstract, complex, evaluative and creative thinking than can typically be fostered in the everyday classroom. Teachers coordinating activities for such groups must be aware of the special needs of gifted students and of appropriate strategies through which these can be met. School staffs as a whole must support the programme and see it as a supplement to, and not as a substitute for, suitable differentiated provision for gifted students in the classroom.

Withdrawal programmes in the UK vary greatly in organisation, effectiveness, and content. The better programmes tend to result from a bottom-up, in-school stimulus rather than from an LEA-imposed, from-the-top-down approach. Nevertheless, Ontario in Canada and Western Australia and Northern Territory in Australia have well-run, efficient programmes that constitute the basis of much positive work. New South Wales has had for many years its Opportunity 'C' programme – full-time, self-contained classes for gifted children within its primary phase.

Residential extension and enrichment courses offer a valuable and unique experience which for many children have been their salvation. Essex LEA's Curriculum Extension Project ran week-long Residential Extension courses from 1972 (primary) to 1978 (secondary) to 1990 and trained over 100 teachers through its working parties in the skills required for lecturing on the courses and for preparing the resources to be used on them. The education consultancy, GIFT, has continued where Essex left off (using the Essex LEA-trained staff as lecturers) and has run day, weekend and week-long courses since 1990. One or two other education authorities have run smaller-scale, pilot courses for short periods but have lacked in effectiveness because of the inadequacy of the lecturers' training. The outcomes from the Essex Project (Whybra 1989) and the GIFT Curriculum Extension Courses have proved extremely beneficial. Children reported gaining in self-confidence on their return to school from the course, of being far better able to confront their ability and the problems it had caused them at school. They were reassured that there was nothing wrong with being clever, that they were not alone (that there were others with similar experiences), and that there was nothing mentally wrong with them:

> I met people like myself who wanted to learn and did not tease me. The workshops offered me new material that was exciting and stretching and the

tutors were prepared to answer lots of questions even late at night! At school, GIFT courses provide a glimmer of hope – they make up an essential part of my studies giving me new subjects to think about and the realisation that I am not alone. They have given me a lot more confidence to be able to socialise and to be able to study new subjects unaided.

They have made me realise that my dyslexia is not a hindrance to increasing my knowledge and they've allowed me to achieve without my writing problems getting in the way. They've given me increased confidence and decreased isolation.

The speed of learning was much faster, but because the courses are so specific, it is possible to look at things to a real depth – at which point subjects (which were boring things learnt to pass exams at school) suddenly come to life and make you want to find out more just for the sake of it. I feel that the courses have made a lasting difference in the way that I look at the work that I do which makes it easier to do. (Gifted students in Whybra 1998)

Through student networking, children have also learnt from their intellectual peers the skills to cope in the classroom with both chronological peer-group and teacher pressure. They have also formed firm friendships with those geographically distant, whom otherwise they would not have encountered socially. Schools reported that children who had been 'switched off' from education had undergone character transformations or had learnt to 'exploit' school life for what it could do for them. We should note:

A talent will be developed if it produces optimal experiences… We can say with some certainty that enjoyment of a student's talent-related work was one of the most important determinants of whether the student developed his or her talent. Optimal experiences are important to talent development partly for this reason: memories of peak moments motivate students to keep improving in hopes of achieving the same intensity of experience again… It is perhaps encouraging to know that a few moments in a person's past can have such an energising effect. (Csikszentmihalyi *et al.* 1997, pp. 252–3)

One interesting value-added advantage was that the lecturers themselves said that when they returned to their schools their own teaching styles had changed for the better. Access to, and opportunities for, experimentation with more challenging, more thought-provoking processes and activities encourage wider usage. The means of stretching and stimulating gifted children are equally applicable to the stretching and stimulation of all abilities. Better teaching, better schools and happier children result.

Principles underlying preparation of work

As regards the basic underlying principles which should govern the teacher's preparation of enrichment projects for gifted children on such courses, it should be attempted to include (Tempest 1974, Whybra 1989):

- an intellectual challenge through the quality rather than the quantity of work. It should be of an interdisciplinary nature, demand the highest standards, and be beyond the school syllabus either through 'lateral' breadth enrichment or through 'vertical' depth enrichment, or through both (Dehaan and Havighurst 1961);
- opportunities for self-direction and independence of thought and action and for leadership and communication skills to develop;
- opportunities for originality and imagination to be demonstrated through problem-solving, creativity, sensitivity, logic and reasoning. If possible the material should be open-ended;
- opportunities for the child to receive individual attention and the chance to discuss options with peers, lecturers, and other adults; and
- an opportunity to access primary sources or first-hand experiences together with extensive reading lists, should the student so desire.

Freeman (1991, p. 208) reminds us that:

> Encouraging creative thinking means giving children permission to play with ideas, however odd, without criticism for a while, and giving time for them to ferment. It is that precarious balance between psychological safety and freedom which allows the child to feel both secure and free enough to take charge of putting forward unusual ideas.

Personal expression must be encouraged and eccentricity tolerated. The lecturing should be informal with mutual respect and opportunities to talk and argue freely; the presentation should lend itself to an informal approach (and not just for informality's sake). There should be no pressure but self-pressure.

Heightened self-esteem produces a more efficient use of intelligence. Self-esteem is nurtured through emotional security and a stress-free environment. The growth of intellect thrives therefore in an atmosphere of secure, well-balanced relationships. The lecturer should engender trust (not familiarity) and a feeling of group well-being. S/he should be prepared to set the problem, to supply the information, to sit back and to let the children come up with solutions while acting as a sort of senior co-learner:

> I learned not to believe automatically whatever people say but to explore subjects from different angles. There is more than one way of doing anything.

> ... each answer was right in its special way and every idea was respected. (in Whybra 1998).

Enrichment is not a matter of the students giving the right answers and being taught, it is more a matter of their asking the right questions and learning how to learn:

> Talented teenagers liked teachers best who were supportive and modelled enjoyable involvement in a field. Students said that such teachers demonstrated an abiding concern for them, could be counted on for support and stimulation and cared about their interests. Teachers represent, for many students, the first encounter with an adult from a particular field of talent. Whether or not a teacher is sensitive and comforting and in touch with a young person's interests tells [students] much about the kind of adult they may be working with somewhere down the line, and the kind of adult they themselves might become. Thus the issue of integration involves a teacher's modelling a professional identity that will be attractive to students. (Csikszentmihalyi *et al.* 1997, p. 249)

Recent Department for Education and Employment policies and initiatives, while trying to give a theoretical boost to the necessity of providing for gifted students, have fallen wide of the mark in practice. The resulting pilot summer school day classes and in-school or LEA initiatives are using untrained staff; ill-defined and inappropriate content (sometimes simply drawing on subject matter from the syllabus for a higher year group); unsuitable materials and resources; and traditional teaching methods and styles. These represent invalid and undifferentiated programmes for gifted students such as those found by Braggett (1985) in his study of enrichment provision in Australia, or as described by Stanley (1979). They are resulting in confusion, disappointed children and a situation where schools/LEAs can claim to be taking action in this field and can be seen to be doing it, rather than actually achieving anything effective. This does not represent genuine extension and enrichment, nor a well-thought out, planned and adequate response to the problem of provision. The encouragement of success and the celebration of achievement per se rather than mute acquiescence in the 'dumbing down' of society will result in positive attitudes toward education, schools, and responsibilities toward society. How a society defines giftedness and attempts to recognise and nurture the talents of those who by its definition are termed 'gifted', says a great deal about the social, political, economic, and psychological health and values of that society. How that society rewards and honours its successful citizens will reflect on its ability to recognise, nurture and produce future talent. The positive effects of celebrating achievement must not be underestimated, neither must the negative effects of not doing so.

The educational and psychological welfare of gifted and talented students in the UK, and the mechanisms by which schools and LEAs control and make the most of that welfare, are too important to become 'spin'-worthy political PR footballs or cosmetic educational afterthoughts. This chapter has tried to address some of the difficulties encountered by gifted children in this country; some of the responses schools can make; some of the contributions enrichment and extension courses can provide in terms of furthering effective teaching, reinforcing students' motivation, developing a positive self-concept, promoting self-fulfilment, and transferring new-found attitudes to mainstream learning; some of the emotional, social and intellectual benefits arising from such courses; and some of the wider implications involved.

'I finally found a place I could fit in.' (Gifted student in Whybra 1998)

It is time that parents, teachers, governors and schools dismissed anti-academic culture and 'dumbed-down' political chimeras and met the educational challenge of enabling our ablest students to realise their potential.

References

Benbow, C. P. and Lubinski, D. (1996) *Intellectual Talent*. Baltimore, MD: The John Hopkins University Press.

Braggett, E. J. (1985) *Education of Gifted and Talented Children: Australian Provision*. Canberra: Commonwealth Schools Commission.

Csikszentmihalyi, M., Rathunde, K. and Whalen, S. (1997) *Talented Teenagers: The Roots of Success and Failure*. Cambridge: Cambridge University Press.

Dehaan, R. F. and Havighurst, R. J. (1961) *Educating Gifted Children*. Chicago: University of Chicago Press.

Department for Education and Employment (1999) *Advisory Group on Gifted and Talented Children: Constitution, Ways of Working, Remit and Terms of Reference*, GTAG4/1 Annex B. London: HMSO.

Feldhusen, J. F. (ed.) (1985) *Toward Excellence in Gifted Education*. Denver, CO: Love.

Foster, W. (1986) 'The application of single-subject research methods to the study of exceptional ability and extraordinary achievement', *Gifted Child Quarterly* **30**(1), 33–7.

Freeman, J. (1991) *Gifted Children Growing Up*. London: Cassell.

Gross, M. U. M. (1993) *Exceptionally Gifted Children*. London: Routledge.

Gross, M. U. M. (1994) 'Responding to the social and emotional needs of gifted children', *Australasian Journal of Gifted Education* **3**(2), 4–10.

Hollingworth, L. S. (1942) *Children Above IQ 180*. New York: World Book Company.

Renzulli, J. S. and Purcell, J. H. (1996) 'Gifted education: A look around and a look ahead', *Roeper Review* **18**(3), 173–8.

Rogers, K. B. (1991) *The Relationship of Grouping Practices to the Education of the Gifted and Talented Learner.* Storrs, CT: National Research Center on the Gifted and Talented.

Stanley, J. C. (1979) 'Identifying and nurturing the intellectually gifted', in George, W. C., Cohn, S. J. and Stanley, J. C. (eds) *Educating the Gifted: Acceleration and Enrichment.* Baltimore, MD: The John Hopkins University Press.

Tannenbaum, A. J. (1983) *Gifted Children: Psychological and Educational Perspectives.* New York: Macmillan.

Tempest, N. R. (1974) *Teaching Clever Children.* London: Routledge and Kegan Paul.

VanTassel-Baska, J. (1998) *Excellence in Educating Gifted and Talented Learners.* Denver, CO: Love.

Wallace, B. (1981) *Teaching the Very Able Child.* London: Ward Lock.

Wallace, B. and Adams, H. B. (eds) (1993) *World-wide Perspectives on the Gifted Disadvantaged.* Bicester: A. B. Academic Publishers.

Webb, J. T., Meckstroth, E. A. and Tolan, S. S. (1983) *Guiding the Gifted Child.* Columbus, OH: Ohio Psychology Publishing Company.

Whitmore, J. R. (1980) *Giftedness, Conflict and Underachievement.* Boston: Allyn and Bacon.

Whybra, J. (1989) *Report on Essex Curriculum Extension Project.* Essex: Essex LEA.

Whybra, J. (ed.) (1998) *Survey of Responses from GIFT Curriculum Extension Course Participants.* Unpublished survey.

Winiarski-Jones, T. (1988) 'Adolescent peergroups: their formation and effects on attitudes towards education and academic performance', *Research in Education* **40**, 51–8.

CHAPTER 4

The role of the family

Susan Gomme

Social and emotional needs are somewhat like the chicken and the egg. It is hard to know which comes first, more especially during the very early part of a child's life. From the beginning, children will react to their social context out of their own emotional make-up and situation. A very hungry new-born baby, for example, is unlikely to respond positively to an attempt to stop him crying with coos, cuddles, tickles or kisses. The appropriate offering, to him, is food. A few weeks later, however, if the former have been the regular precursors to feeding, his response may be modified from intense frustration to pleased anticipation. So the pattern of social interaction, the way in which messages are sent, received and responded to, is formed progressively out of a series of encounters with whatever 'others' a child is in contact with. These others, in their turn, will bring an overt or hidden emotional content to the encounter, to which the child will react.

It is probably not important whether we put social before emotional or emotional before social, as long as we recognise that they are equal partners in a complex process of understanding the self in relation to the world and in deciding, on the basis of that understanding, what is an appropriate way to behave. Simply because the phrase 'social and emotional' seems to have become a standard formula, I believe that there is a danger of falling into an unthinking assumption that social needs come first and emotional needs must, in some way, be modified to fit them, or attended to as an afterthought. It seems to me important, therefore, to recognise that the beginnings of socialisation come well before a baby has any real understanding of separateness and therefore of relationship to other people. Even if the carer brings a powerful socialising agenda, for example in wanting to impose a regular feeding routine, the baby's responses are, to begin with, pure emotional reactions.

Genetic considerations

Where does the emotional development of a child begin? The prime building blocks must be in the unique genetic inheritance from both parents which will mark an individual character from birth. Most parents of more than one child will notice differences between them from the start. Why does this particular baby cry so constantly? Why is she so intolerant of any sort of disturbance or discomfort when her brother, whom they believe they treated in almost exactly the same way, was generally placid and good-humoured?

It is helpful (though, as so often, very difficult amid the pressing demands of small children) to recognise her awkwardness as part of the definition of her personality: she is not going to sit down under adverse circumstances, but will do what she can – in this case screaming is her only option – to bring about some improvement. Her nature is to take action in a situation where her more thoughtful brother might be aware of other issues, needs or signals from outside. Where she screams about her mother's failure to meet her need, he, by contrast, is aware that there is also a satisfaction in waiting until his mother is able to give the attention willingly.

Family members who claim to see likenesses to older generations, although often partial in their observations, may be offering a useful pointer here. I have known two grandmothers each competing to attribute to the other the stubborn determination of their two-year-old granddaughter. It was, in fact, probably inherited equally from both; but what the argument did was to offer her parents the reassurance that this somewhat intractable behaviour was within the family norms. It also indicated, to some extent, how such a characteristic might develop into adulthood. Presumably the way they dealt with it will have been guided, at least in part, by their inter-relationship with the relatives concerned. Did they value, and therefore reinforce, it or did they find it unacceptable and try to persuade or discipline the child into modifying or suppressing it?

Of course that will only have been one of many in an intricate blend of inherited traits. It is easy to affirm and enjoy those seen as desirable; harder to accept those which have already caused difficulty or distress to other people in the family. Even more difficult are the characteristics, inherited or learned, which the parents find most unacceptable in themselves. Nevertheless, the most important emotional input the family can give is to welcome this new member as someone with a unique personality and a right to an individual identity.

Even in a new-born baby this identity is not entirely genetic. Much work has been done recently on the effect on the foetus of the mother's physical and emotional state during pregnancy. Nowadays expectant mothers are encouraged, variously, to eat wholesome food, avoid smoking, alcohol, nuts or blue cheese in order to assure their child's physical health. They are also told to be relaxed, happy, sing to their babies and welcome them at birth. Much of this might seem to be simple common sense, but it does have the virtue of encouraging the family to look forward to someone special. But, as we have already noted above, the baby's innate emotional make-up will have a considerable bearing on how this exchange develops. The mother also needs response and returns for her efforts if the contact is to grow fruitfully. This will be easier if the family does not start out with the assumption that babies are unprinted raw material, to be trained into a pre-ordained system of development and behaviour. The social relationship starts at birth and demands recognition that both partners in it are uniquely themselves as much as they are alike and share many common features. Initially, it is the adults who must draw on their experience and understanding to accommodate the baby.

Beginnings of socialisation

After the trauma of being born, being forced out from dark, temperature-controlled containment into light, space and atmosphere – which is the physical event of becoming separate from the mother – emotional development depends initially on a prime carer, generally the mother. To begin with, being completely helpless, the baby's physical and emotional well-being is inextricably linked with the quality of that care. The way in which the basic needs for nourishment, safety and warmth are met will form the foundation of the child's subsequent development, as represented in Abraham Maslow's (1954) Hierarchy of Needs (see Figure 4.1, p. 55). The underlying emotional response accompanying such simple tasks as feeding, washing and keeping a baby warm and safe will reinforce particular styles of communication. Babies who are generally welcomed, smiled at, talked to and cared for before they become aware of discomfort are already developing a basic feel-good factor on which to build their sense of self-esteem. Those who are driven to crying before their needs are met will be more likely to assume that this is the most reliable way of getting the comfort and contact they crave. A lengthy discussion of this primely formative relationship can be found in John Bowlby's seminal work *Attachment and Loss* (Bowlby 1997/8).

Gifted children are no exception, but are often endowed, from a very early age, with a greater awareness of the emotional function of such exchanges. A few hours after the birth of her son, a mother told me, 'I looked into the cot to see what I'd got, and he looked back to see what he'd got.' He was, of course, displaying the precocious motor control often observed in gifted infants, who are regularly reported as focusing early, talking early, walking early and above all very aware of the external world. It is precisely this unexpected quality of reaction from the child which may encourage, undermine or distort the social interaction, depending on the way in which the family responds, or the flexibility of their social norms.

A baby girl, less than a week old, was heard crying in the bedroom upstairs. 'I'll go and see', said her grandmother reassuringly to her exhausted mother, 'whether I can settle her again.' A moment later she came down, astonished. 'I'd swear that child could understand what I was saying. I just told her it was all right, we were still here and she could go to sleep again. I didn't touch her and she couldn't see me by the door, but she shut her eyes and went to sleep.' For that family, the event set a style of reassuring communication that could be developed according to need. So, for example, when this daughter started primary school, she could discuss its drawbacks with her mother and come to some acceptable resolution of them. This serves as a diagram of the bedrock of love, acceptance and affirmation within the family that gives the child a safe footing while dealing with outside difficulties.

From the beginning, then, it is clear that gifted children are no different from any other children in their basic needs. Where they may differ is in the ways that these may be expressed by them or acceptably met. Margaret Branch, one of the prime movers in founding the National Association for Gifted Children (NAGC), used to observe in talking about them that a gifted child was 'an ordinary child plus' and that they had 'one skin less'. Take the example, for the ordinary child plus, which I have quoted of the mother encountering her new-born son. She had expressed, in a nutshell, one of the most common experiences faced by the parents of gifted children. In quite unexpected ways, they challenge expectations, assumptions and norms. From the outset, they ask to be seen as individuals. The hypersensitivity, or 'one skin less', is often demonstrated by a quite exceptional awareness of general emotional mood. This is not to claim, of course, that such children are necessarily fragile or demanding of special treatment. How the child understands or acts upon this awareness will depend greatly on his emotional resources and social surroundings.

The way in which this behaviour is received progressively sets the pattern for further social interaction. The differentness can be welcomed and enjoyed, so that the child develops a warm sense of being appreciated and can continue to offer freely what is currently interesting, absorbing or disturbing. Often this is, in any case, irresistible. Who could fail to be enchanted by the comment, from a toddler observing the iridescence of starlings, that 'they are called starlings because they have so many stars on them'; or another who announces seriously that 'giraffe has two fs in case there are two giraffes'. More difficult, perhaps, until you recognise that it is invested with much less emotional 'baggage' than you might be carrying, is the four-year-old boy's concern: 'When Daddy dies, before we bury him we must take the money out of his pockets'. The baby girl who so surprised her grandmother by apparently understanding what she said, held the following conversation with her mother shortly after starting school: 'Mummy, I have a problem'. – 'Oh, what is it?' – 'Well, Mrs Smith says when we are learning the words of a song, I must go on repeating it with the rest of the class even though I knew it the first time through.' – 'I see. That is difficult. I wonder what we might be able to do about it?' – A brief, thoughtful silence follows, then: 'I know. I'll do this.' So she took up her position, feet apart and hands behind her back, mouthing the words silently. The solution was practical, amusing and offended nobody, but it let her off what she saw as an unreasonable task. Who would have expected a five-year-old to come up with it? Her creative response, however, was made possible by the family culture of open discussion. Had she not been encouraged to talk things out as they affected her, she probably would not have been able to work out the solution.

Exceptional development

At a training weekend for NAGC counsellors we studied the four standard areas of developmental progress in young children, namely: physical, intellectual, emotional and social. With specific reference to their experience of gifted children, I asked the group to consider these in relation to Maslow's (1954) Hierarchy of Needs and to colour-code the steps of the pyramid accordingly.

Physical was to be brown, emotional red, social green and intellectual blue. In theory it should have been a nice, neat diagram, with a physical base and a smooth progression to the pure ether of intellectual satisfaction at the tip. In fact they found it very hard to avoid splurges of all colours at every step and, at the end of half an hour, none of them had completed the second part of the exercise – which was to cut the pyramid into its separate elements and rearrange them in a typically 'gifted' hierarchy. Their conclusion was that, in the gifted children of whom they had experience, developmental (and consequently emotional and social needs) were often highly atypical and overlapped each other in many ways. They quoted examples of children for whom the answers to questions were more important than eating, or who would rather create something than have friends. For others, they said, logic and justice were paramount and overrode appeals to consider other people's needs and feelings. Even more than the rest of us, gifted children present a pattern of emotional and social development which is not tidily linear but amorphous: a sort of very flexible sphere whose surface erupts into unexpectedly sharp points in some places and fails to expand appropriately in others. Patricia Mason and Juliet Essen make the same point, reinforcing it with reference to Susan Leyden, in a survey conducted among NAGC members in London:

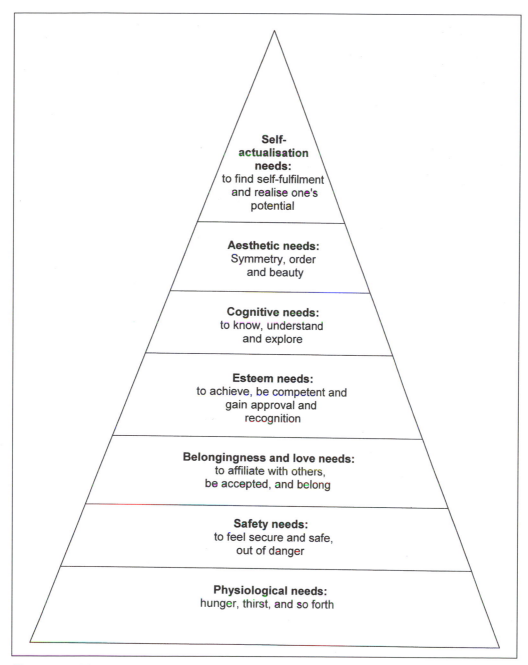

Figure 4.1 Maslow's Hierarchy of Needs

The child who reaches developmental milestones very early will, like other children, receive encouragement and praise from parents, but the parents' feelings may well be mixed: amazement with apprehension, pride with a degree of uncertainty as to what was happening, welcome edged with dismay… This mixture of feelings, this confusion of response, will be transmitted to the infant and form the beginnings of deeply troubling feelings' (Leyden, in a discussion document dated 1981). He begins to feel he is unusual and this leaves him feeling uncomfortable. As soon as comparisons are made, which happens early in an infant's life, there is no niche into which he can fit, as other infants can. Children of his age are less advanced in ability or intellectual development or understanding, but older children may be more advanced in their social or physical development. (Mason and Essen 1987, p. 3)

'The trouble with her', remarked a teacher friend to the parents of a seven-year-old, 'is that she doesn't know what age she is.' She was in the throes of a temper-tantrum because her older brother and sister refused to let her play tennis with them. Small wonder: she was not big enough or well enough coordinated to make an acceptable contribution to their game, but they had all just been involved on level terms in a hand of cards and she generally took an equal part in any family discussion. So her age, within a brief time-span, had ranged from, say, emotionally four and a half (screaming and kicking in inarticulate fury) through seven (in terms of chronological and physical development) to 14 or 15 (in her intellectual competence).

'The high intelligence and reasoning powers of these children', as Mason and Essen (1987) go on to say:

was clearly not always able to help them to understand emotional issues. For some … their parents found their child had relatively more need to talk about feelings and behaviour, and the child could be greatly helped by doing so. Others, however, although often very sensitive and aware, seemed particularly unable to express their emotions verbally and resorted to giving vent to their feelings on the furniture or the doors instead (p. 34).

Such disparity between different aspects of a child's growth is difficult for everyone to manage, and most of all for the child. To say of the girl described above, 'you can talk to her like an adult' may be to put expectations on her which make it even harder for her to reconcile those conflicting elements. If the approval she gets is for 'being like an adult', how can she come to terms with the violent and childish frustrations which are also part of her make-up. Let us hope such children can be contained within the safe structure of a loving family which will understand the predicament without condoning unacceptable behaviour.

Further developmental gaps

Susan Leyden details other gaps or mismatches in development which give rise to emotional predicaments (Leyden 1985). A second is the mismatch between the child's desires and the ability to achieve them. The more clearly a child can see a blueprint for a scheme, the harder it is to tolerate their physical limitations. One mother was driven to contact the Samaritans because she could not cope with her toddler's extreme tantrum. The cause? He could not draw two eyes symmetrically in the face he was painting. The difficulty in most of these cases is first to recognise the cause of such intense frustration and secondly to find a strategy with which to manage it. It takes considerable strength of purpose for parents to remain calm and to contain the situation when their child is in the grip of such strong negative emotion. The insight to recognise that it is not simply wilful misbehaviour or 'attention seeking' (to quote that commonly used rag-bag of disapproval) is an important first step. In her book *Children in Need* Sula Wolff has a salutary maxim in this regard: 'The symptom is a message in disguise' (Wolff 1987, p. 36). If we do not understand the message we may be offering quite inappropriate treatment for the symptom.

A variant on this situation occurs when the frustration arises, not through the child's physical limitations but from the mismatch between external expectations (generally related to age-norms) and the child's true ability. The mother of a five-year-old, teaching her daughter to knit, was mystified to be asked to cast on 13 stitches for her; some time later the child remarked triumphantly that she had now knitted 143 stitches. How did she know? because she had just completed 11 rows, the child replied. This was not quite the level of numeracy to which she was being introduced at school at the time, when rote-learning of tables was not part of the curriculum. Here the family obviously, even if unconsciously, was providing the sort of culture in which the child could follow her interests outside formal schooling. So were the parents in the case of the seven-year-old whose father was congratulated on his child's progress by his class teacher: 'he has borrowed *Charlie and the Chocolate Factory* and is steaming ahead with it. Isn't that great?' 'Well', replied the father, 'he has been through *The Lord of the Rings* twice already at home, and is now working on the appendices to understand the geography and language structure which Tolkien has created.'

In the second instance we can see the advantage of close contact between home and school. The teacher already recognises this as an exceptionally able child and makes the opening for the parent to add his own observation of the extent of that ability. But this relates more to his intellectual than to his emotional development. How do such children relate emotionally to others of their own age who do not share their preoccupations and interests? One boy of five, interviewed by an educational psychologist because he seemed to lack social skills, complained that the children in his class were boring. Why was that? 'Well, they don't read *The Spectator*', he replied, 'so I can't talk to them about what I find interesting in it.' Is it fair to expect them to cope unaided with a considerable degree of developmental discrepancy, either within themselves or between themselves and their age-peers *and* conform to an expected behavioural and social norm? I believe it is very important to recognise the extra difficulties they may be encountering at the same time as making it clear that these do not provide an excuse for unacceptable behaviour. In working with musical children, Michal Hambourg, the NAGC Music Counsellor, makes a point of responding to whatever performance they offer with affirmation and praise before she goes on to discuss with them what they find difficult or discouraging. At this point she will often play for them a piece which incorporates a considerable degree of related difficulty. She will then tell them how much hard work and practice it took her to master the techniques necessary to achieve such a level of performance. For many gifted children, for whom most of the things expected of them, especially early on in their development, appear to come very easily, such an approach may be the first introduction to the need for persistence and commitment. The important thing is that it is not punitive in tone. Asked how she set about teaching her child discipline, one mother of four said, succinctly: 'First of all, when he is little and helpless, I'd give him everything he needed. Then I would say "I love you, but I say no".' In this way she was already making a distinction between the person and the deed, so that the child did not grow to believe that he was only loved for what he did.

Praise of the person through the achievement is regularly seen by our counsellors as a particular pitfall in the social development of gifted children. It is all too easy to fall into the trap of apparently only approving when they achieve at a high intellectual level. The ubiquitous phrase 'good girl/boy', rather than 'well done', can easily lead intellectually advanced children into a false analysis of their general situation, especially if they are lacking in social skills. At its extreme, the logical progression is to the devastatingly destructive summing up of one highly intelligent, and up to that point highly achieving, university student who had just failed his first exams: 'Of course I realise that I am only socially acceptable in so far as I succeed academically'. One can see how such a conclusion might be built up from entirely well-meaning individual comments or unspoken positive feedback. People are nice to me and praise me when I am clever but laugh at me or worry about me when I am clumsy or fail (to ride a bicycle or play football, for example); so I'll keep on doing the things they are nice about and ignore the things I am teased or criticised for. But this pattern underlines my (probably now repressed) sense that I am an oddity, failure or cause for concern. So, when, inevitably, the day comes for my intellectual achievement to fall below my expected high standard, I become a non-person: I simply have nothing else to offer.

Family stresses

Many parents seem quite astonished at the idea that even quite small babies can absorb and react to unexpressed feelings in those around them. The more these are concealed, the more possible it becomes for the child, who after all has no in-built encyclopaedia of the ramifications of human psychology, to misinterpret the discomfort they produce. And the younger the child, the more egocentric the interpretation is likely to be. I have known children who have believed that their bad behaviour caused their fathers' long absences or separation from the family. Or others whose parents' concern at their lack of social skills have led to a sharp downward spiral in their own self-esteem, which, in its turn, increases their friendlessness. Even if it was not true in the beginning, the perception that they are socially inept becomes a self-fulfilling prophecy.

Most discussions of good parenting agree on the basic principle that the related negative emotions of anxiety and guilt are the most undermining of constructive family input. A sensitive child may well interpret these feelings as being her or his fault, even if it is the parents who actually believe they are failing in some way. This is particularly true if there is no discussion about where or why the anxiety or guilt arises.

In this respect it is the parents, as much as the children, who need to be freed from unrealistic expectations. The comforting concept of being a 'good enough' parent is probably not good enough for their image of how they should be. Add to this the common anxiety of knowing how to cater for the exceptional needs of a gifted child and the unexpressed worry in the household may well be at a high level. There is a great burden of responsibility, especially if the idea of having a gifted child is completely unexpected or the gifts fall outside the family experience, in making decisions about providing for the specialist education which may be required. The cost to the family in time, energy and commitment as much as in finance may be extreme. Some parents move house, take on extra work commitments, spend early mornings, evenings and weekends ferrying the child to extra classes or coaching, to accommodate their child's growing demands for special training or equipment. One hard-pressed couple said of their highly musical daughter 'If we didn't love her so much, she would be better off if we gave her to a family who could offer her the musical background of which we have no understanding.' Of course the conditional clause is absolutely crucial here. What they can and do offer her is the essential support, security and human warmth and understanding which will inform her interpretation in musical performance. Since then they have all come to recognise that this is the absolute bedrock which nobody else can provide. They have also realised, tacitly at least, that parents, like everyone else, have limitations and make mistakes. It is much harder for children to face and accept their own finiteness if they are offered no family model for it.

This particular family have at least the simplification of having only one child, and of seeing themselves primarily as being there to cater for her growth into maturity. The situation becomes much more complex where the parents themselves have work demands which place a heavy call on their resources, or even more where there are siblings whose needs and interests conflict with those of their gifted brother or sister. Families often go out of their way to offer 'equal' treatment to other siblings, only to see the gifted one take possession of that activity as well. One couple, recognising that they seemed to be neglecting their elder son, decided to take him for swimming lessons. As they had no babysitter, his gifted younger brother was taken along too, but on the clear understanding that the lessons were not for him and he was to occupy himself without interfering. He disappeared, and father, mother and coach concentrated on the older boy. After a while, looking up to check where he had got to, they saw him at the end of a diving board, from which he executed, quite untaught, a very competent dive. 'Who is that?' asked the coach. 'I must have him. He's an absolute natural.'

It is not always easy to avoid resentment of the apparent cuckoo in the nest and to demonstrate that the care for all of them is equal, even though the distribution of resources is apparently unfair. The way in which these tensions are handled may make a considerable difference to the child's perception of her or himself and so to the degree of pressure to succeed at all costs. Learning to share is as important as learning to succeed or be best and the family ethos is the safest situation in which to learn it. It depends, in essence, on a respect for the contribution that every member of the household brings to the family, on affirmation of what s/he does well and constructive criticism of the things that are out of line or distressing to other family members. In this, as in most things, openness is generally the most productive approach, especially in allowing an airing of difficulties or resentments before they become inflamed.

Ground rules

Many parents are thrown into confusion by their gifted child's ability from a very early age to manipulate or argue against the (probably unspoken) rules of the household. Where this situation arises it is important to work out the basic ground rules which suit their particular family, spell them out clearly and keep to them consistently.

It is surprising how often such rules are completely unspoken, until one reflects that they are learned, as is one's native language, by a process of gradual, unanalysed assimilation. So, when they start to talk their assumptions through, mother and father realise that, from the point of view of family rules and upbringing, they themselves come from very different families of origin. They have to start, therefore, by agreeing between themselves which rules hold good for them and for this generation. But they must take into consideration what is right or manageable for the particular individuals in the family. Is it fair, for example, to insist that a toddler whose sleep requirement is less than normal must lie in a darkened bedroom with nothing to do because bedtime has traditionally been set for 7 p.m.? Even if, quite reasonably, the exhausted parents need time on their own, the child might be allowed to play quietly in the bedroom, or read until overcome by sleep. Many such situations can be resolved by discussion and negotiation, even at a very early age, but the parents need to be aware of the child's level of interest and understanding. Life, death, power, possessiveness, control and impatience with the demands of society are common preoccupations for these children (Gopnik 2000) and we do them no service by denying their right to address them. Sometimes their conclusions are astonishing.

Anthony, in the reception class at school, believed he was superior to his brother James, the elder by 18 months. When Anthony announced that he was king, James, after some consideration asserted that he was emperor. Anthony promoted himself to being head of a neighbouring empire, so James threatened war and conquest. During that week the reception class was introduced to the creation story. Anthony, recognising his brother's greater size and strength, decided on a private satisfaction of his ambition; late that night his mother overheard him saying quietly, in the privacy of his bedroom, 'In the beginning, Anthony…' In our experience, it is not uncommon for children who have such logical skill to believe, at this age, that they will be able to control the world as soon as they have mastered the systems by which it operates. Recent research in Britain and the United States demonstrates that such capacity to reason comes considerably earlier in childhood development than we tend to assume (Richardson 1999, Gopnik 2000). The way in which this belief is modified and brought into a socially more acceptable, not to say realistic, expectation depends most of all on the way it is handled by the family. A supremely self-confident primary-school child may be irritated by her father's regular dictum 'You are not the only pebble on the beach', but the image provides a constant reminder of the huge number of people who have claims on the world's resources, and will return to her when she has the emotional resources to recognise the fact.

It is often observed that sibling rivalry is the best introduction to the competitive reality of the adult world. Here, like young animals from the same litter, children can try their strength and skill against one another without being allowed to inflict any serious harm. As with so many family situations, this is true to the extent to which the conflict is safely contained within the family structure. No parent can be completely dispassionate about such struggles, but it is important to be aware of one's own predispositions before reacting. One may have a natural sympathy for the child who has the same emotional make-up or who occupies the same position in the family. Are you more aware of the unfairness of being the eldest, for example, or do you sympathise with the younger one, who is always being compared to the one who is so well-behaved or has achieved so brilliantly? Your subconscious reaction may, even if it seems perfectly justifiable, reinforce a sense of injustice in the child with whom you feel less in tune. To acknowledge that as a factor is part of introducing your children to the reality of living. The understanding that life is not even-handed or fair, but different in some way for each of us, is a better preparation for socialisation than a scrupulous attention to equal shares. Parents may not be prepared to reinforce this lesson by deliberately cutting unequal slices of cake and handing them out at random, as I have heard of in more than one family, but there are still plenty of in-built inequalities, which can be recognised and talked about.

In the same way, it is important to recognise your own unresolved agenda and the possibility of trying to achieve satisfaction or acclaim through your gifted child. There is the world of difference between driving a gifted young person to achieve what you would have liked to do and allowing her or him to define the goal before offering all the encouragement and support you can supply. In other words, you need to be able to recognise what is motivating you as well as doing your best to identify the right direction for your child. 'Difficulties', says Sula Wolff, 'arise when the child's qualities of temperament conflict with the parents' expectations of how he ought to be' (Wolff 1987, p. 72). This is as true, though the clash may not be so overtly dynamic, if the child is temperamentally pacific and conforming and the parent ambitious and goal-orientated as it may be the other way round. In particular, a multi-talented child may allow her or himself to be driven along a career path which is chosen by parental assumptions or agenda. Professional or highly academic parents may not even realise that their very clever children have an intense, inner creative urge which is more important to them than the perceived success of becoming a doctor, judge or professor.

Keeping the balance

Where the child has a single-minded ambition, identifying the best upbringing may at least be a straightforward process. It becomes much more difficult in the case of a multi-talented one. Keeping the balance between achievement and relaxation, between hours of study and some measure of healthy leisure time, may be a serious worry for parents. Once again, the best principle must be to allow the child, as far as possible, to set the agenda, but at the same time to be aware of parental responsibilities in terms of good health, physical safety and the requirements of law. Crossing the road when one is too small to see the traffic approaching over the brow of the hill may be a simple example, but sometimes has to be demonstrated to an independent-minded toddler who believes she understands the principle and can put the required code into practice. If, instead of insisting that she must do as she is told, one can take the first opportunity of lifting her up to see the oncoming car which was not visible to her, she is much more likely to recognise that you are caring for, rather than unthinkingly restricting her.

The foundation of such one-to-one discussion can also be used when it comes to the understanding of wider social issues, where the limitations have to be drawn for the average rather than the individual. This is often a very hard piece of learning for the gifted reception-class child, for example, and the family can do a great deal to help the transition from negotiation for what suits one personally to the understanding of what the rules have to be for thirty of us. Concrete examples, like the importance of obeying traffic rules, can help even a very young child to recognise that there must be accepted norms where there are too many people to accommodate individual tracks without unacceptable clashes. Acknowledging that such restrictions may be necessary may be the first step to accepting that the social norms can be beneficial as well as boring or frustrating. It offers an opening for the child to explore where is the best place to be in relation to society.

This exploration often veers from one extreme to another, as the individual comes to grips with conflicting social and emotional needs. The need to be oneself, to satisfy the special desires and develop as far as possible the special abilities one has, is often an isolating experience, especially if one is out of step with one's age-peers. But the need to belong and communicate is just as strong, and pulls in the opposite direction. Gifted children who deliberately under-achieve at school, in order not to be ostracised or picked on, need understanding and support rather than scolding. If they are being forced into an invidious choice, at least they have shown that they want the social contact and are prepared to make a sacrifice for it. Those who are driven further and further into an intellectual world of their own, because they can find no satisfactory way of relating to people who do not think like them, are probably in a more difficult position. In either case, the family is an essential resource in finding whether they are happy with the choices they have made or in supporting them in what may be a long process of finding their place in the world. It often takes years for one or more aspects of development in such children to integrate into a complete person, at ease with himself and the world. In the meantime, the family has to bear the stress of watching what may well seem an extreme form of growing pains. They also deserve as much help, support and understanding as possible in order to offer a positive and supportive environment for as long as may be necessary.

Because gifted children are extremely variable in their interests, emotional characteristics and achievements, it is very hard to offer any generalised formula for caring for them, especially since what is manageable will differ also according to individual families and their needs and reactions to the situation. For this reason, it is often helpful for the parents to be able to talk through and come to terms with their own needs and feelings, so that they may be better able to offer to their child the best possible environment for growth. Someone who is not directly involved in the family but who can help to make a clear analysis of where the problems are centred and what resources are available is often very helpful in identifying possible ways forward.

The aim, always, must be, by consistent affirmation and appropriate social framework, to help these children to believe in themselves enough to reach out, explore the frontiers of their understanding and bring to joyful fruition their innate creative abilities. The process is often protracted and demanding for the whole family, but the result is immeasurably rewarding for all of us.

References

Bowlby, J. (1997/8) *Attachment and Loss*. London: Pimlico Press.

Gopnik, A. (2000) *How Babies Think*. London: Weidenfeld and Nicholson.

Leyden, S. (1985) *Helping Children of Exceptional Ability*. London: Routledge.

Maslow, A. H. (1954) *Motivation and Personality*. New York: Harper and Row.

Mason, P. and Essen, J. (1987) *The Social, Educational and Emotional Needs of Gifted Children*. London: Cicely Northcote Trust.

Richardson, K. (1999) *The Making of Intelligence*. London: Weidenfeld and Nicholson.

Wolff, S. (1987) *Children Under Stress*. Harmondsworth: Penguin.

CHAPTER 5

Gifted and talented children with dyslexia

Lindsay Peer

Intellectual potential, represented by the abilities of individuals, is a social, cultural and economic asset that no nation can afford to neglect. Equal opportunities and anti-discrimination legislation encourage the entry of talented but disabled students into higher education. When the existence of a legally-recognised disability such as dyslexia obscures the recognition of able individuals by institutions of higher education, the individual, educational institutions and the nation lose. (Singleton 1998, p. 1)

Commonality between the groups

Were it not for the many examples of highly able and even gifted adults who are also dyslexic it might be difficult to conceive of dyslexia and giftedness co-existing. Dyslexia is an 'invisible disability'. Those who are affected by it may well make strenuous efforts to disguise the fact; so it can be with giftedness. The two have much in common regarding their effects: both may make children feel 'different'; both may cause 'important others' to relate to them initially in inappropriate ways; both may cause the growing child to develop differently from his/her peers, often causing social and emotional difficulties.

It is a common assumption that attainments in one area give a good indication of likely attainments in most other areas, and may even show how 'bright' a person is. Gifted learners with dyslexia can think, talk and reason about concepts perfectly well although they may have significant difficulty reading and expressing their highly developed ideas on paper. They will often be aware that there are other learners about them who cannot think and reason to anywhere near the same level, yet because of their superior level of literacy skills they will present as higher achievers in the daily school curriculum. Having poorer basic skills and a limited number of ways open to them for demonstrating awareness, perception and information, gifted dyslexics have to fight to have their considerable knowledge base and abilities recognised. In order to be accepted as successful they may need to 'prove' themselves over and over again to their teachers, some of who are in any case not attuned to the idea of this specific special need. To achieve full academic, social and emotional potential, a high level of motivation and self-esteem has to be maintained and demonstrated throughout the long years spent at school. Under this level of sustained pressure, there can be many circumstances that contrive to cause them to drop out along the way.

The gifted child can reason, perform, understand and talk about her/his particular area of excellence at adult level, but still be a child emotionally and socially. Adults often do not know how to handle such disparities in gifted young people particularly if they themselves are dyslexic. Both giftedness and dyslexia can affect the way children think about themselves; how they 'fit' into their peer group and what kind of person they may ultimately become.

Another area of similarity is that of adult decision-making of a far-reaching nature influencing their lives in a profound way. For instance, if a child shows musical ability, in string playing, good and competent tuition and quite extensive practice must take place from a very young age, certainly by six or seven years old. An adult must decide whether this should or will happen. Similarly, if a child shows literacy difficulties based on a dyslexic-type difficulty; structured, sequential, multi-sensory teaching, as well as the skills development so necessary for the young dyslexic learner, will need to be put in place early on if the child is not to fall behind at school. Dependence, therefore, on adult decision-making is heightened for these children. If parents and teachers are not empowered and knowledgeable, even the gifts of creativity and thinking can be lost leaving the young learners frustrated, unsupported and highly vulnerable.

Finally, the very existences of both conditions have been matters of heated debate until quite recently. The word 'belief' was even used in relation to both of them: *What is dyslexia? What is giftedness? How do we identify both conditions? Do we treat such children in the same way as others? Are they children with special needs? The two cannot possibly exist side by side!*

There are many overlaps and a great need to ensure that educators are trained, that the public are aware and that appropriate policy is in place at local and national level.

Perspectives on dyslexia

Historically, there were those who doubted the very existence of dyslexia. There were no doubt many reasons for this, not least the fact that it is not easy to physically recognise the disability. The very suggestion that any of these 'failing learners' could also be gifted was out of the question – totally beyond belief. However, even a 100 years ago, there were researchers in the fields of health, education and science who recognised the condition, although in not as advanced a way as we do today. Initially some suggested that dyslexia was 'word deafness', others 'word blindness'. There were yet others who suggested that it was minimal brain damage or a result of emotional problems.

However, both dyslexia and giftedness are now grounded on a much firmer research and practice basis. Indeed, in his address to the Orton Dyslexia Society in 1982, Geschwind spoke about their relatedness (Galaburda 1993); suggesting the possibility that, together with the deficits related to the affected area of the brain, certain lesions could result in 'superior functions' in the unaffected hemisphere and may explain the superior right hemisphere capacities exhibited by dyslexic children.

He went on to discuss learners with hyperlexia, who, despite their apparent high ability in reading aloud, showed mediocre comprehension: conceivably accounted for by the fact that the area implicated in the learning of graphemic-phonemic conversions was appropriately developed, but its connection to other brain regions was deficient.

Since that time much research has been undertaken in the hope that we would understand the neurological differences present in the brain of the dyslexic learner. Centres such as the Institute for Behavioural Genes, University of Colorado and the Neurological Unit at Harvard Medical School have been highly influential in our understanding of the biological condition. Notable British researchers in the fields of education and psychology have contributed much to the furtherance of our understanding of the genesis of dyslexia. People, such as Frith (in Frederickson and Reason 1995), Snowling and Stackhouse (1996) and Hatcher (1998), have written at length about the phonological background to dyslexia with recommendations for intervention: Stein and Talcott (1999) have studied visual perception; Fawcett and Nicolson (1994, 1999) have offered a complementary aetiology relating to the influence of the cerebellum on the automisation of motor and language skills; Reid (1998) has written on cognitive functioning in dyslexia and methodology for good practice; and Turner (1997) has contributed to the debate on cognition and assessment.

The results of this body of research have been successfully translated into educational practice in many countries. Teaching programmes that encompass multi-sensory methods based on the work by Samuel Orton in the 1930s, have influenced individual teaching programmes, e.g. Alpha to Omega, Dyslexia Institute, Hickey and Kingston and, more recently, on whole class adaptations (Johnson *et al.* 1999). What, however, is clear and exciting is that Geschwind's initial hypothesis of highly able right hemispheric learners has been borne out. There is much evidence that dyslexic learners may still have high abilities in the visual and creative fields (West 1991). We need only look at the colleges of art and design; at the university departments producing superb dyslexic dramatists, architects and engineers. They are all highly able, creative learners developing their abilities and adopting strategies to cope with their difficulties.

Identification

Giftedness is not a precisely defined concept. It can refer to the highest levels of competence in a given field that may be artistic or sporting or intellectual. Alternatively, it may refer to a person with a very high level of ability in many areas, sometimes referred to as a 'polymath'. There are even people who have referred to giftedness in terms of very highly developed social and/or interpersonal relationships. Terman (1925) and the 'Intelligence School' refer to individuals with an IQ of over 150 as being gifted. I feel that the term is best reserved for the person whose abilities and attainments are qualitatively different from the majority. Indeed it should be remembered that Carlyle (1795 to 1881) defined genius in the following way: 'Genius which means first of all transcendent capacity for taking trouble'.

Within this chapter I use the term 'giftedness' to describe children who have outstanding ability in one or more specific areas of the curriculum, far and beyond those of their peers – a term reflecting current understanding of intellectual development. It is more than just having a high IQ. Indeed the testing of IQ is problematic in determining absolute overall scores for both gifted and dyslexic children (beyond the problems of IQ testing per se). Often the results produced show a significant disparity between verbal and performance scores. Either may be particularly high. Therefore attempting to give an average score is not only against test procedures, but would be highly misleading. It is the examination of those very components assessed in the sub-tests that highlights the cognitive patterns the child manifests and hence leads us into an understanding of the appropriate educational provision incorporating learning styles. This disparity of abilities and weaknesses led to the description of dyslexia being synonymous with *specific learning difficulties* although current research has revealed that dyslexia is only one such difficulty. It highlights the fact that there are many areas in which these students excel while concurrently experiencing substantial weaknesses. It is this disparity of ability that is the warning light to the educator and parent. It is this that makes the child so potentially stimulating and exciting to teach and mentor. It is this that causes problems when badly handled.

We need to separate out those with a general learning difficulty, those who have had poor teaching in a particular key area or who are demotivated for a variety of other reasons, such as boredom with the National Curriculum. Such children also need support, but not the same as those with a *learning disability*. Gifted dyslexic children need a balanced approach in both promoting strengths and in recognising and supporting difficulties. It is, therefore, highly appropriate to consider curriculum-based assessment in their identification as they move through the system. We need to ask ourselves many questions when trying to identify the strengths and weaknesses of a child, many of them being beyond the basic literacy and numeracy processes. The answers should point to appropriate learning styles that will ultimately lead to greater access and success in a variety of subject areas.

It is common for many dyslexic children to have a significant weakness in areas of *organisation*. This can affect them in life-skills as well as in schoolwork. As they get older and the demands grow, the pressures cause substantial difficulties. For those in the gifted dyslexic group, there is an additional pressure – that of a need for perfection in the area of their excellence (Parker and Mills 1996). Unfortunately this can be coupled with a complete lack of interest in their standard of performance in areas they see as irrelevant. This can even apply to communicating what they have learned to others. The motivation comes from personal knowing and/or doing. They can live in an isolated world of their own making. There is direct conflict here where many dyslexic youngsters find themselves unable to reach the level that they feel they so badly need yet are resistant to even considering the standards of others. If 'perfectionism' refers to having high standards, a desire to achieve, conscientiousness, or high levels of responsibility, eventually it can become a virtue not a problem. However, in a child it is a problem that frustrates and inhibits achievement. Teachers must therefore be aware of the need, sensitively, to direct and support so that frustration and obsession do not set in. There may also be a very real problem in that the National Curriculum assumes a 'balanced curriculum' following a particular year-by-year sequence. Many gifted children just don't see it that way!

Speed of Processing of both the written and, in many cases, the spoken word can cause difficulties. The problem here usually relates to the processing of the *input*. The child has to convert the words s/he hears into understanding. Only then can it be processed to determine an answer. There is usually no problem with this internal processing. They are not 'slow-thinkers' just 'slow-receivers'. Unfortunately this may mean that a teacher has gone on to the next question by the time the child's answer emerges! This time delay may often be misinterpreted as lack of knowledge. A reprimand can follow. The listener simply cannot process many instructions spoken at speed. Material not chunked into sequential phrases can cause the child to be totally bewildered – very frustrating for a child who is highly able.

Similarly, when given written work to comprehend, s/he may well be struggling to decode words, and therefore miss the sense of the passage. Should that child have understood the content, the answers to any subsequent questions would have been given readily. Identification of a processing difficulty will immediately separate out those children with a learning difficulty and those with other problems in learning.

Short-term memory weaknesses are common amongst dyslexic children. These must never be confused with low IQ, but unfortunately often are. Remembering times tables and formulae was a nightmare for a dyslexic lecturer I know with a PhD in mathematics. He told me that he even took a calculator to go shopping and did not know his two times table! One should not confuse an inability to remember with an inability to process concepts. Likewise, children often have great difficulty remembering spellings given to learn – teachers can easily assume that no effort has been made and again the child is in trouble.

Sequencing is problematic for some. The history student who wrote about Henry IV rather than Henry VI and got zero marks for the essay is a good example. Remembering how to arrange items as requested; organise a bibliography and produce a good essay can be complicated for the person with the greatest amount of knowledge. In the English essay, the author that confuses 'no' with 'on', 'was' with 'saw', is having as much as a problem as the one who confuses 'b', 'd', 'p' and 'q'. The one who cannot use a dictionary or thesaurus effectively is significantly hampered in secondary school.

Laterality is a great difficulty for some, with great confusions between right and left. Think of the child who is removed from the sports hall because s/he 'misbehaves' having run the wrong way; the child who gets confused in mathematics when doing long division. Think of the driver who can't find the way from A-Z and can't read and then think of the child who cannot memorise a map in the geography class.

Remediation

Metacognitive processes need to be taught to the student as s/he gets older in order to deal with weightier demands. Study-skills will become invaluable for success in higher level work. Problems become evident in the taking of notes in lectures, the preparation for examinations and the balancing of heavy homework schedules. All students would benefit from this although these students cannot manage without them.

Dyslexic learners traditionally have weaknesses in reading, writing, spelling and sometimes numeracy. However, all of these weaknesses can exist in a person who is highly able, knowledgeable and very creative. So, what is it that teachers need to do? It is critical that such children are identified as early on as is possible in their school careers, if not before. There are tests and checklists now available that can identify children at risk as early as three years old (Nicolson and Fawcett 1996, 1998). We no longer have to wait until children fall behind and their self-esteem plummets. What is vital is that alongside the early identification process is a programme that develops the prerequisites for learning that are so necessary for the acquisition of the literacy process, the key to the curriculum. For the older learner there are many programmes available, which are suitable for parents and teachers to work with and support the child.

Multi-sensory teaching programmes have proven themselves internationally over many years and can be used to teach reading, spelling, grammar, and punctuation as well as foreign languages, numeracy, etc. However, unfortunately this is where the two conditions can react against each other. Multi-sensory teaching to alleviate dyslexia requires regular, detailed teaching, review, practice and overlearning. It enables the child to function better, it does not produce a 'cure'. As I pointed out earlier, paying any, let alone detailed, attention to areas of the curriculum which are not of direct relevance to the main interest or expertise can be anathema to many gifted children. It takes a special sort of expertise to engage them and the motivation and materials must be directly related to their aspirations. Generalised statements of potential future good will cut no ice at all!

It is vital that teachers and specialists monitor the detailed progress being made in each curricular area by these children on a regular basis. They need realistic targets but by definition these may be wildly disparate. The brighter the child the higher the expectation should be. It is unacceptable to expect that the target for a gifted child to be at the level of the class average. Depending on the profile of their excellence such expectations may be above or below that average. Teachers must also be aware of the implications of all test results. A score in a spelling test when no automaticity is required, is not going to be relevant when the child is working in the context of writing at speed in examination conditions when there are many other things to think about at the same time. Likewise, accuracy in a spelling test may not transfer across the curriculum without substantial extra work on the part of the teacher. Regarding reading tests, teachers must look at the relationship between that which they are testing and the demands of the curriculum. For example, a single word reading test will not give an indication of the speed, accuracy and comprehension of a piece of text.

Policy in the UK (DfE 1994) currently requires that Special Educational Needs be recognised and that Individual/Group Education Plans be developed to meet each of those needs. *Differentiation* is about the presentation of materials at a high academic level in a way that makes them accessible to all children. There is nothing about the intellectual level of the information that needs simplifying, just the way in which it is presented. Educationalists, psychologists, parents and policy makers also recognise the need to watch out for indications in behaviour that are signals of distress. The child who closes down is as concerning as the child who plays-up. The relationship between stress, dyslexia and giftedness has not been touched upon a great deal in the literature; but the issues are very real.

The question we need to pose, therefore, is to what extent should we address a child's emotional struggles with the learning process as well as the academic process itself? If children feel alienated from learning they are bound to feel strain. Policy makers often do not seem to value the process of learning, only the achievement of reaching set targets. In such a climate some children are being set up to fail. School is not a voluntary option for them, however hard things get, so there is no way out. The one thing we need to do and so often fail to do through lack of time is to listen to the child and see beyond the behaviour to the cause. However, if we are to truly work in a system which values inclusive education for the vast majority of children, we must be aware of the needs that go beyond the process of the acquisition of literacy. There is no doubt in my mind that a child's level of intelligence may influence her/his emotional and behavioural responses to persistent failure, teacher and parent expectations, self- and peer-group expectations and ultimately remediation. These are highly able children who should be brought into the process; speaking to them and explaining the issues can be a great help. So often we have a tendency to speak over the child's head, about, rather than with, her or him. Congdon's (1981) guide for young people goes a long way to addressing the situation.

While we would all agree that the ability to read and write effectively is highly desirable, for some, through no fault of their own despite excellent teaching, it will be difficult to achieve those skills. On the bright side, we must also note that we are entering a new era; that of technology. Computers will read to those who need that level of help, and write upon command for others. The language produced will be appropriate and accurate. For highly able dyslexic learners, computers will remove the areas of difficulty leaving them free to develop the areas in which they perform best – the ideas, the creative and innovative thinking. This in turn will lead to the success that is so rightly theirs – high motivation and positive self-esteem – leading to a positive self-fulfilling prophecy.

Consequences of inappropriate behaviour

Despite the level of knowledge that we possess these days, there is still a great shortage of training for teachers in the identification, assessment and remediation of gifted dyslexic learners. As a result, there can be dire consequences if teachers employ inappropriate attitudes towards such students.

There are many gifted learners who, whether or not they are dyslexic, have spent years unidentified or mishandled in the classroom. As with dyslexia, inappropriate methods of teaching, low expectations due to apparent poor functioning, bullying in its various forms all lead to immense frustration, low self-esteem and often deviant behaviour. Work by researchers such as Miles and Varma (1995) on stress and dyslexia, and Alm and Andersson (1995) on prisoners with dyslexia, have more recently highlighted these issues. Their findings indicating that large numbers of those on probation and in the penal system have low levels of literacy, yet high levels of creativity, show that questions need to be asked as to the relationship between giftedness, dyslexia and delinquency. Might it be that such young people are more vulnerable because they don't 'fit in' and perform in ways that might be expected of them? Is it that these children have greater perceptual acuity and are more sensitive to environmental factors than others? Do they desire the material successes that appear to be available to others so much that they easily find alternative ways of achieving their desires if success along an acceptable academic route becomes impossible? Were they frustrated by knowing that they were able and being treated as slow? All these situations lead to high levels of frustration and anger.

Then there are others who are faced with levels of frustration which, while not leading to deviant behaviour, do still prove problematic to the individual. As examples, Van Gogh, who only sold one painting during his lifetime, and James Joyce, who had his book, *The Dubliners,* rejected by 22 publishers before it was accepted, must have suffered significant degrees of stress. Whatever the reaction, there is no doubt that stress is endemic when the gifted are not recognised. How much more so when we add in a learning disability.

Students talking

Riddick *et al.* (1997) quote several students at university who have lived their lives with dyslexia, many of them identified late in their academic careers:

Caroline – Question: *Has dyslexia affected your self-esteem?*
Not knowing what dyslexia was did. People just think you are stupid and it makes you feel stupid. And not to know you are dyslexic, outside academic work, it makes you feel less sure about yourself. I wasn't really confident until I was about 15 or 16. Then I got to college and thought that it doesn't matter any more. (p. 98)

June: *Statement:* I would often cry and want to run out of the class because it was just too painful. They just laughed, even the teachers laughed. (p. 78)

Peter – Question: *Have you ever met anyone in the past who has ridiculed your dyslexia, and, if so, how did you cope with the situation?*

At school lots of teachers ridiculed it constantly. At secondary school I had two periods of French and two periods of German which I had to sit through and those teachers didn't know my problem with English of course. It doubled up and trebled up and quadrupled up because you went to different teachers for different subjects and each teacher tended to ridicule or say things which would tend to add to it and I became just numb to it, but particular things do stand out, but they stay in my conscious memory and [are] not relegated to an unconscious mind, which needs something to switch them on. I remember them in the front of my mind and they come to me quite often and I dream about them. I keep dreaming about being back at school and being told that I am lazy, stupid and silly and if I don't learn to read and write I won't be anything. I won't get a job, I'll never learn to drive, I'll probably be on the streets sleeping rough. When I left school I remember walking down the drive from the school and feeling elevated at leaving school, as if I'd left prison, looking back and saying 'I'll never enter this place again', but looking forward with great fear about how would I cope in adult life. It was very scary. (p. 74)

Avoidance of failure is possible

Neglect could be easily avoided if educators were aware of the issues in their broadest sense; were able to identify gifted dyslexic students, assess their needs and make appropriate provision early on in the education process. What it is that causes one person frustration that is painful but manageable, and what it is that causes another to spiral down into unacceptable behaviour we do not know. However, what we do know is that gifted dyslexic learners can be identified early on and need to be if we are to avoid the levels of stress that can so badly affect them and the community around them. As McLoughlin (1994) states:

> The often unsympathetic attitude and behaviour of other people undermines confidence and contributes to the development in many dyslexics of profound and deeply ingrained low self-esteem … An effect of low self-esteem and lack of confidence is to reduce or eradicate the motivation to do anything, which is then interpreted by others as well as by the individual as further evidence of low intelligence. (p. 49)

There are those who continue to suffer through misdiagnosis or bad handling and these must be high on our list for observation at home and at school. So, what should we look out for as signs of danger in our children at school or beyond?

Childhood Depression, according to the Learning Disabilities Association (LDA) – K12 Mental Health Subcommittee manifests itself in the following ways:

> Personality change: angry, irritable, moody; change in appetite – usually loss; change in sleep patterns – difficulty in going to sleep; waking up earlier; loss of energy and general feeling of lethargy; loss of interest in friends, play, activities, sport – often say that nothing gives pleasure; low self-esteem: 'I'm dumb, ugly; no-one loves me; I have no friends'; difficulty in making decisions; difficulty concentrating (not Attention Deficit Hyperactivity Disorder); shows feelings of helplessness, possibly speaking of suicidal thoughts: 'Life is not worth living. I would be better off dead. Sometimes I think of killing myself.'

Thankfully, most do not take such drastic steps but many do suffer from low emotional ebb much of the time. The awareness of the ingredients of self-esteem must, therefore, be made known to all that live or work with children as these can add to or detract from the quality of life:

- Physical safety (watch for the children who are being bullied at school, verbally or physically)
- Emotional security (difficult when the child senses himself as a 'loner')
- Identity (Who am I?)
- Affiliation (Which groups do I belong to? Who am I like?)
- Competence (Can anyone recognise my competence at anything?)
- Meaning (Does my life have meaning? Where will I end up? Can I cope?)

I truly believe that the best teaching in the world will not work if the children do not have their emotional needs met first.

But it does not have to be this way. There are others who, despite their difficulties, have gone on to become tremendous successes. As West (1991) tells us:

> It is no longer unusual for some parents to realise, after their children are diagnosed, that they themselves have long suffered silently with some form of learning disability … many affected parents appear to be among the most successful in their fields, having worked out elaborate strategies to capitalise on strengths and to disguise or discount areas of weakness … Anecdotal evidence, suggesting some form of general pattern, is often considered interesting or amusing material for family stories and is passed down as family lore from one generation to the next. Such patterns can be traced in a number of the most prominent and best-documented families. (pp. 17–18)

In West's list of gifted dyslexics, he cites among others: Hans Christian Anderson, Albert Einstein, Thomas Edison, Leonardo da Vinci, King Karl XI of Sweden and William Butler Yeats.

There is clear evidence that, when school provision is right and families have had successful gifted dyslexics in them in previous generations, the chances are that the children will go on to do well. There are others who despite all difficulties go on to achieve great successes.

If we are working and/or living with the stressed youngsters, the following are some strategies that might help:

- Communicate clearly ensuring that words and body language match. Believe that what you are saying will work.
- Give only positive directions: re-focus on what you *want them to do* and not on the unacceptable. (Try telling the boys not to look at the girl outside in the mini skirt and concentrate on their maths. What do you think they will think about?!)
- Always build up hope. I believe that the emotional state of mind is at the heart of our successes, emotional, social and academic. Watch out for learned hopelessness. When things have got really bad, such children and adults become vulnerable.
- Always give encouragement and be specific about the small steps of success.
- Take the blame and don't blame the child for something misunderstood. Processing problems get in the way and it is up to us to find alternative ways of explaining.
- Watch the language you use so that you do not collude with their negative images of themselves. We are good at catching them doing things wrong, but not so good at complimenting them for doing things right. So, catch them being good and give compliments wherever possible.

This would, ideally, go alongside a change in the school situation where one would see a focus on the giftedness being developed rather than only on the learning difficulties being addressed; where the gifted dyslexic child would be placed in a high flying class because s/he can understand the concepts and intellectually function at that level rather than in the bottom stream because s/he cannot spell. I would hope to see specialists trained in both the needs of the gifted as well as in an understanding in the needs of dyslexic children. These specialists would be able to prepare support lessons to suit. I look forward to a time when all class teachers are able to recognise the strengths of the child, give extension materials and differentiate for the child where the literacy difficulties impede progress; when the gifted dyslexic is used to explain concepts and impart knowledge to other children in the class despite having poor literacy skills and when role models of older gifted dyslexics can be introduced to these children to boost them forward.

Conclusion

I believe that the vast majority of gifted dyslexic children are still unidentified in schools today and those few who have been identified are in the main not receiving appropriate provision. There is a great need to highlight the existence of this group and make provision for them at local and national level. The worst thing for them is to place them in classes with under achievers as this is bound to cause severe stress in an already difficult situation. Ideally, they should be in a group with others like themselves so that the 'disability' is put into proportion and the giftedness is highlighted. Specialist teachers need to be fully aware of and trained to deal with their social and emotional needs as well as their academic ones. Raising self-esteem and influencing motivation must be high on the list for training programmes. (Perhaps this should be provided for all children – but that is the subject for another chapter elsewhere!) In theory, there should only be a small number who would benefit from a highly specialist school provision – those whose needs are so severe and complex that they cannot be met in mainstream school. However, until resources are in place to deal with this exceptional group, many of them will simply suffer in school.

At the heart of the Waldorf method of teaching (Hutchinson and Hutchinson 1993) is the belief that education is an art. His educators believe that an artist is not so much the one who paints, draws, sculpts or dramatises, but is the one who is the *visionary*. Our children with their dual exceptionalities are also so often the visionaries; take away the shackles and the gifts are clear. Teachers need to be looking out for children who display characteristics of giftedness in a variety of areas: creativity, curiosity, multiple interests, self-initiated learning and so on. They must not be put off by the fact that these very bright children are slow to acquire literacy; this often masks the giftedness. There is always a good reason for this disparity of ability. Teachers will need to be trained and resources put in place; even classroom practice may need to change if we are to identify hidden areas of potential giftedness. All gifted learners, dyslexic or not should and could be joining the ranks of the successful. They have the qualities and the ability, if only we could identify them and learn how to nurture them effectively. The uniqueness is there – it is our role to find the way forward.

Bibliography

Alm, J. and Andersson, J. (1995) *Reading and Writing Difficulties at Prisons in the County of Uppsala.* Stockholm: National Labour Market Board of Sweden.
Congdon, P. (1981) *Dyslexia: Towards a Better Understanding.* Solihull: Gifted Children's Information Centre.

DfE (1994) *Code of Practice on the Identification and Assessment of SEN*. London: HMSO.

Fawcett, A. J. and Nicolson, R. I. (eds) (1994) *Dyslexia and Children: A Multidisciplinary Perspective*. Hemel Hempstead: Harvester Wheatsheaf.

Fawcett, A. J. and Nicolson, R. I. (1996) *The Dyslexia Screening Test*. London: Psychological Corporation.

Fawcett, A. J. and Nicholson R. I. (1999) 'Developmental dyslexia: the role of the cerebellum', *Dyslexia: International Journal of Research and Practice* 5, 155–77.

Frederickson, N. and Reason, R. (1995) 'Phonological assessment of specific learning difficulties', *Education and Children Psychology* 12, 6–17.

Galaburda, A. M. (ed.) (1993) *Dyslexia and Development: Neurobiological Aspects of Extra-Ordinary Brains*. Harvard: Harvard University Press.

Hatcher, P. J. (1998) *Sound Linkage: An Integrated Programme for Overcoming Reading Difficulties*. London: Whurr Publishers.

Hutchinson, J. and Hutchinson, H. (1993) 'Waldorf Education: a program for gifted students', *Education of the Gifted* 16(4), 400–19.

Johnson, M., Phillips, S. and Peer, L. (1999) *A Multi Sensory Teaching System for Reading (UK Edition)*. Manchester: Manchester Metropolitan University.

McLoughlin, D. (1994) *Adult Dyslexia: Assessment, Counselling and Training*. London: Whurr Publishers.

Miles, T. R. (1983) *Bangor Dyslexia Test*. Cambridge: Learning Development Aids.

Miles, T. and Varma, V. (ed.) (1995) *Stress and Dyslexia*. London: Whurr Publishers.

Nicolson, R. I. and Fawcett, A. J. (1996) *The Dyslexia Early Screening Test*. London: Psychological Corporation.

Nicolson, R. I. and Fawcett, A. J. (1998) *The Dyslexia Adult Screening Test*. London: Psychological Corporation.

Parker, W. D. and Mills, C. J. (1996) 'The incidence of perfectionism in gifted students', *Gifted Child Quarterly* 40(4), 194–9.

Reid, G. (1998) *Dyslexia: A Practitioner's Handbook*. Chichester: Wiley.

Riddick, B., Farmer, M. and Sterling, C. (1997) *Students and Dyslexia: Growing up with a Specific Learning Difficulty*. London: Whurr Publishers.

Singleton, C. H., Thomas, K. V. and Leedale, R. C. with Horne, J. K. and Plant, R. R. (1997) *CoPS 1: Cognitive Profiling System*. Beverley: Lucid Research Ltd.

Singleton. C. H. (1998) 'Report of the working party on dyslexia in higher education', *Dyslexia in Higher Education: Policy, Provision and Practice*. Hull: University of Hull.

Snowling, M. and Stackhouse, J. (1996) *Dyslexia Speech and Language: A Practitioner's Handbook*. London: Whurr Publishers.

Stein, T. and Talcott, J. (1999) 'Impaired neuronal timing in developmental dyslexia – the magnocellular hypothesis', *Dyslexia: International Journal of Research and Practice* 5, 59–77.

Terman, L. (1925) *Genetic Studies of Genius,* Vol. 1. Stanford, CA: Stanford University Press.

Turner, M. (1997) *Psychological Assessment of Dyslexia.* London: Whurr Publishers.

West, T. G. (1991) *In the Mind's Eye: Visual Thinkers, Gifted People with Learning Difficulties, Computer Images and the Ironies of Creativity.* Buffalo, NY: Prometheus Books.

CHAPTER 6

Culturally diverse gifted students

Stan Bailey

It is accepted that children from cultures that are minorities within any society are likely to be under-represented in special provisions for the gifted and talented, and that is even more likely if they are from low-income families (Frasier 1993, Tomlinson *et al.* 1997). Reasons for this include schools using inappropriate (i.e. culturally insensitive) methods of identification and the students' inability or unwillingness to respond positively to teaching that does not closely match their cultural values or learning styles. Under-achievement is both cause and consequence of this identification problem, particularly where identification relies upon subjective judgements. If allowed to go unchecked, it provides superficial 'evidence' for the negative stereotypes that some teachers have of particular cultural groups, and Frasier *et al.* (1995, p. 7) cite a range of research which 'indicates that students, teachers, and school professionals continue to have low academic expectations for culturally and linguistically diverse students'.

There are many 'masks' behind which potential talent may be hidden and it is an unfortunate irony that gifted students are sometimes highly adept at using these talent masks. Understanding the masks and helping students to feel able to discard them is the challenge for teachers, parents and anyone else seeking to provide an education process that will develop to its full the potential of all students, regardless of social or cultural background.

The nature of the challenge

Maker and Schiever (1989) identify a sense of powerlessness as a major inhibitor of talent development in students from culturally diverse backgrounds. Causes of this powerlessness are said to include:

- the perception that success requires complete emulation of majority culture standards, even when different from family standards;
- the lack of a sense of belonging when changes to achieve success in the majority culture result in lack of acceptance in either culture because the minority culture views the change as denial of one's heritage, and the majority culture continues to view the individual as physically and historically different; and
- the perception that certain successes are unimportant or not valued in society and in school. (p. xvi)

To address these, and to develop the culturally diverse students' feelings of personal liberation and empowerment, Maker and Schiever (1989) offer the following suggestions:

- increasing 'ownership' of the school experience;
- building cultural 'bridges';
- maintaining and developing bilingualism;
- developing the student's sense of self-worth and potential through experiences with role models and mentors;
- involving families in the setting of educational goals and the design of educational programmes for their children;
- developing the perception that teachers *really care* about children's success; and
- avoiding stereotypes, negative expectations, and the behaviours that imply they exist. (pp. xvi–ii)

Being identified publicly as highly able has social as well as academic consequences for students. In a frequently cited article, Gross (1989) identifies a 'forced-choice dilemma' facing gifted students, the choice being between peer friendship and school achievement. In cultural groups that value affiliation, or where feelings of connectedness are seen as important for self-preservation, this pressure to choose affiliation over individual achievement is likely to be even stronger. At the very least, there is a tension between these, as Van Tassel-Baska *et al.* (1994) note:

Culturally diverse groups battle internally a dual value system message: one that calls for a sub-group loyalty and adherence to tribal, family and cultural traditions, and the other that calls for individual excellence in a mainstream world. (p. 190)

Ford (1995, p. xi) echoes this point when discussing the sacrifices and risks (of rejection, misunderstanding, isolation and alienation) that gifted African-American students face if they are to pursue the realisation of their high potential. Elsewhere (Ford 1996) she advocates that class teachers use group work and cooperative learning tasks to promote social interaction between minority students and their white peers: 'Time spent in shared and non-competitive activities can encourage friendships and decrease students' fears, stereotypes, and feelings of social isolation' (p. 81).

Finding unobtrusive ways of affirming students' giftedness without making them feel embarrassed about it is another strategy teachers should consider – for example, private comments such as 'Your contributions today were very creative' or 'You were the only one to think of that idea', but also via communication with their parents, to help strengthen the home/school/student triangle as a positive and supportive one. An example of culturally specific expressions of talent being sacrificed to acceptance into the dominant culture is found in a paper from New Zealand. Asian refugee children who arrived in New Zealand, proud of their traditional art work, were observed to replace their unique Asian style with illustrations more akin to those of their new host country after entering school there (Lee 1994, cited by Rawlinson 1996, p. 353).

Helping culturally diverse students to become conversant with the ways of the mainstream culture, particularly its schooling, is a way of empowering them to participate in it to an extent of their own choosing. Doing this in a manner that does not cause these students to devalue their own cultural background (or family) is the challenge teachers should accept as a central issue for schools to address. Day (1992) has commented on the importance of this in his investigation into the success of some Australian Aboriginal students in the senior years of high school, in the face of a pervasive negative stereotype. The successful students remained 'very proud of their Aboriginal culture and heritage' while also acquiring 'some school and Western cultural knowledge and attitudes which are important for success at school' (p. 24). In similar vein, Modood (1992, p. 82) commenting on integration within British society, recommends that the 'positive role of ethnic pride' should not be overlooked.

For some culturally diverse gifted students the challenge of maintaining a positive allegiance to their cultural heritage, while also developing their talents through school-based forms of enrichment or extension, may prove daunting, especially if such extension programmes are viewed with suspicion or disfavour by their ethnic peers. In this situation, it is important that counsellors or pastoral care advisers provide support that will complement, or, if necessary, substitute for, that from school or home. Colangelo (in Delisle 1992) recommends that whoever provides this support should be aware of the five stages of ethnic identity proposed by Banks and should be encouraging culturally diverse gifted students to develop through these stages toward a balanced acceptance of self and others. The stages are:

Stage 1: *Ethnic Psychological Captivity* – individuals who internalise negative stereotypes of their culture and strive vigorously to become a part of 'mainstream' culture.

Stage 2:   *Ethnic Encapsulation* – individuals at this level interact only with others of their same ethnicity, thinking themselves as superior to other groups.

Stage 3:   *Ethnic Identity Clarification* – individuals who have 'come to terms' with their own ethnicities and begin to interact with various ethnic groups, while maintaining primary affiliation with one's own ethnic heritage.

Stage 4:   *Biethnicity* – individuals who have developed an appreciation for their own and other ethnicities and begin to interact with various ethnic groups, while maintaining primary affiliation with one's own ethnic heritage.

Stage 5:   *Multiethnicity* – individuals who reach this stage have reached the ideal within a pluralistic culture. They function readily within several ethnic environments, appreciating the differences and uniqueness of each. (Delisle 1992, pp. 183–4)

Mentors, and class teachers, may need to discuss explicitly with their students how best to respond to racial abuse, which some children face regularly (Klein 1993, p. 189), and to other negative aspects of the hidden curriculum. Teachers themselves may, often unwittingly (e.g. through their non-verbal, as much as their verbal, messages), communicate to students their preference for some individuals over others. If students 'read' this as a preference for other cultural or ethnic groups over their own, there is a temptation for them to use this assumed slight as a reason, or excuse, for trying less diligently on school tasks. In such cases, it is important that parents do not reinforce this negative, if also understandable, reaction by siding with their child in an antagonistic stance towards the school – for the consequence of this may well become some degree of entrenched under-achievement, if the child interprets this family 'support' as excusing her/him from having to try to achieve at school (Davis and Rimm 1998, p. 294). It has also been pointed out that misconceptions about religious, or other cultural, differences may result in a potential talent being unsupported at school. For example, Duffy (1998, p. 29) notes that it is sometimes assumed that Muslim children are not allowed to depict the human form, whereas it is only in mosques that such depictions are prohibited. Unnecessary frustration may result if restrictions were imposed upon the expression of a Muslim child's artistic potential because of this misconception.

Concern has been expressed at times that the promotion of certain domains of talent in children from cultural minorities may serve to entrench stereotypes about the range of their abilities, for example, it is feared that encouraging indigenous Australian children to develop their high potential in sport, art or music will reinforce the view that these are the only domains in which they are likely to experience such success. Similar concerns have been expressed in Britain about

Afro-Caribbean children's successes there in sport, music and dance (Gillborn 1990, p. 113). This highlights the need for an inclusive identification process which ensures that high potential in other academic domains is not overlooked and that successful adults in these, from a range of cultural groups, are cited as role models whenever appropriate.

Providing support

For gifted children whose cultural differences combine with other factors to increase their risk of under-achievement, it may be desirable for the school to seek ways of countering this by also increasing their resilience - that is, their capacity for remaining competent despite misfortune or stressful events in their lives (Novick 1998, p. 201). A longitudinal study of a multiracial group of 698 children in Hawaii (Werner and Smith, in Novick 1998) found that the resilient children in the group often had a teacher who supported them as a confidant and positive role model, in addition to whatever encouragement they received from their family.

Ford (1995, pp. xvi–xvii) recommends nine guidelines for those wishing to promote positive self-concepts and identities in gifted African-American students. Several of these seem applicable to members of any culturally different minority group, namely:

1. Focus on, and acknowledge, the strengths of these students.
2. Help them to build positive social and peer relations, both with gifted students from other cultural groups and with non-gifted students within their own cultural group.
3. Encourage these students to be bicultural, e.g. so that they understand which behaviours are most and least acceptable in particular social situations.

If, as has been suggested is the case in some American minority groups, each generation of people from cultural minorities becomes better educated than the previous one (Plummer 1995, p. 296) there may be less family 'know-how' of the kind that enables parents of the majority culture to be able to advise and support their children in school and beyond. On the other hand, some cultural minorities continue to provide strong support to help their youth withstand racist slurs and institutional obstacles to personal fulfilment of academic potential, for example, Modood (1992, p. 16) comments on 'Asian self-reliance [and] emotional solidarity' in Britain.

In one secondary school in Sydney, Australia, the teacher with pastoral care responsibility for those students who had been accelerated by single-subject grade skipping arranged a weekly meeting with that group of students to enable them to discuss with each other and with him their progress and any matters of concern. There may be value in schools making similar arrangements for culturally diverse gifted students, to encourage them to act as a support group for each other and to provide regular access to a teacher who is seen to be 'on their side'. Ford (1996) cites a similar example from the USA, where a teacher organised a midday discussion group for gifted students which addressed 'stress, personality styles, testing, recognising strengths and weaknesses, family conflicts, career concerns, and relationships' (p. 81). Butler-Por (1994) states that this demonstration of teacher support is 'most important for creating emotional security, which constitutes an essential condition for overcoming underachievement' (p. 222).

Promising strategies

Hulmes (1989) argues that:

> The future of education in schools (and in other educational institutions) is threatened just as much by soured human relationships which have unacknowledged cultural differences as their common cause, as by low salary levels for teachers, by lack of resources of one sort or another, or by technological developments which may make existing arrangements obsolete. (p. 152)

If so, it is important to use teaching strategies designed to promote empathy, active listening, awareness and tolerance of cultural variety, and respect for individual differences. Those outlined below should help in this pursuit but are only a small sample of promising practices.

Teaching social skills

Goleman (1996) has argued for all children being educated in social-emotional literacy. In a multicultural society, this needs to be broad enough for children to be at least literate, if not fully fluent, in the social-emotional domains of their peers' cultures as well as that of their own culture. Some examples of what this social-emotional literacy may entail are spelled out by Matthews (1999):

> Nurturing relationships and keeping friends; accurately analyzing social situations; having empathy, taking others' perspectives; listening, resolving conflicts, and co-operating; reading social and emotional cues; being able to resist negative influences; and developing leadership abilities. (p. 62)

Several teachers I know have a year-long social skills component built into their regular programme. Usually, this means that they focus on a specific 'social skill for the week', for example, making and maintaining eye contact, paraphrasing others' answers, using acceptable ways of breaking into a group, and, after initial explanation of the skill, they refer to this throughout the week as the need or opportunity becomes evident during normal classroom activities.

A more formal approach to developing cultural literacy may be found in the notion of cultural journalism – a qualitative research approach that students may use to investigate their own school or community. In addition to the research and communication skills that students will acquire, this approach fosters reflection, empathy, values clarification, connecting with one's own heritage and culture, and strengthening intergenerational ties (Matthews 1999, p. 64).

Bibliotherapy

When discussing barriers to effective counselling, Ford (1995, p. xii) notes that 'counselling is perceived by many minority groups as a sign of weakness; going to a counselor brings shame on the family'. If so, this highlights the necessity for class teachers to develop and employ low-key bibliotherapy which involves the use of suitable books to help children work through social-emotional problems or concerns: books where a main character exhibits the same problem(s) as the child receiving this form of personal development. For some children, the use of such a book allows them to confront and deal with an otherwise painful situation by externalising it through the book character. It is like using a puppet or a toy as a 'third person' to help a child look more objectively at an aspect of his or her life. It also may help for children to see that others, whether real people (as in biographies) or fictional characters, experience similar fears or pressures to themselves and to reflect upon the success of the strategies they use to cope with these. Behaviour change is difficult to achieve but may be less so if we recognise that it is not just cerebral but involves feelings as well. Note that, with younger children, it may be more appropriate to use puppets as the filter through which they are encouraged to express their own feelings and recognise that we have choices about how to respond to life's challenges.

Adderholdt-Elliott and Eller (1989) offer some very important practical advice on the use of bibliotherapy:

- The first step is the careful selection of a book that matches the child's needs. School or local librarians may be able to provide suggestions for the teacher or parent in search of an appropriate book.
- It should be recognised that the book is not a 'magic pill' but a catalyst for fruitful discussion between an adult and the child. The child's reading of the book should be followed by talking about its content with the adult who has previously read and thought about it.
- Insight, when the young reader sees a connection between his or her situation and that of the book character, may not occur until some time after reading and discussing the book. That is, incubation or reflection time may be necessary.

- As with any counselling or pastoral care work undertaken by those without extensive formal training, there may be times when the nature of the student's internal conflict or disturbance warrants referral to a fully qualified professional counsellor.

Students who are keen and fluent readers may accept bibliotherapy more readily than others, but a book that is read to a child, by parent or teacher, can be used for this purpose too. Furthermore, teachers can use as class reading matter books that contain material likely to enhance inter-cultural understanding and respect, provided these are first of all high quality children's literature in their own right. Films and videos may also be used in this manner. Bibliotherapy has its limitations as an awareness raising strategy but it does provide one means of addressing the challenge of empathy building among children of diverse abilities and backgrounds.

Night of the Notables

A virtue of Betts' Autonomous Learner Model (Betts 1986) is its inclusion in the curriculum of an explicit social-emotional component. One strategy within this affective strand, 'Night of the Notables', deserves special mention here, for it may be used to encourage appreciation of, and respect for, high achievers across a range of cultures. Students engaged in this activity are asked to choose a notable adult, past or present, whose achievements they admire. Not surprisingly, it is common for teachers to observe that students pick notables who are similar to themselves in personality and interests. Over a period of five to ten weeks the students research in detail the life and beliefs of their notable person, so that on the 'Night of the Notables' – when they each dress and act in role as their notable – they are able to answer searching questions about their notable's achievements and motives when asked by members of the audience of peers, parents, teachers and other community members.

The potential for students to choose their 'heroes' from various cultural groups is obvious and has naturally occurred in some of the Australian schools using this strategy. Students have chosen their notables from a wide variety of cultures, though predominantly their own, and some have even chosen a person of opposite gender from themselves, e.g. a girl who elected to become Nelson Mandela for the duration of the activity. The possibility exists for culturally diverse students to raise the profile of their traditional culture by highlighting some of its talented individuals and their accomplishments, while there is also the potential for students from the mainstream culture to explore another culture through the life of one of its famous people. Night of the Notables is a strategy that encourages students to develop their research skills and extend their knowledge base in a manner that is highly intrinsically interesting for students and audience alike.

Mentoring

One way of providing culturally different students with emotional support is to provide them with mentor and role models from within their own culture who are 'confident, personally secure, and academically and professionally successful' (Ford 1995, p. xiv). This has been done with some early signs of success in Australia where highly able Aboriginal students, aged 10 to 16, have participated in mentoring-at-a-distance programmes using e-mail as the means of initial contact.

Mentoring, where a school student is paired with an adult in an area of mutual expertise and high interest, can be a highly effective way of addressing the intellectual needs of the gifted, but it is often a source of social-emotional support too. Adult mentors can act as role models for coping with frustrations, setbacks and failure, for dealing constructively with success and for social skills of cooperation and communication. In the case of gifted students from culturally different backgrounds, a mentor from within the same cultural group can be a role model for dealing with the challenges specific to being a member of that sub-culture within a culturally diverse society. In some instances this may lead to raised aspirations for school and beyond, as well as coping with any negative pressures to under-achieve for peer affiliation reasons. Davis and Rimm (1998) assert that 'all other treatments for underachievement dim in importance compared with strong identification with an achieving model' (p. 304).

The Anaiwan Project, in the Australian state of New South Wales, provides an example of the positive social-emotional outcomes that can result from mentoring (Bailey and Chaffey 1998). In this project Aboriginal students, identified as having high academic or creative potential, were paired with Aboriginal adults who were role models of achievement within a range of fields. An innovative aspect of this mentoring was that most of the communication between mentor and mentee, over a period of several months, was by e-mail, before the project culminated in a face-to-face meeting at a one day workshop which all participants attended. While it is too soon to know the long-term consequences of this project, the early signs are that it had an uplifting effect on the confidence and aspirations of the students involved, attributable in no small part to its emphasis on developing their appreciation of, and respect for, their cultural heritage, while also communicating with positive role models who were able to empathise with the difficulties they faced along the path to realising their high potential. Frasier *et al.* (1995, p. 9) cite a study of factors 'identified as prevalent in the lives of subjects who had risen successfully out of disadvantaged backgrounds', among these being 'a questioning orientation', 'awareness of alternative paths' and 'supportive, inspiring relationships', all of which may reasonably be expected to be encouraged or provided in a positive mentoring relationship. Some cultures have traditionally had an approach similar to mentoring as their way of dealing with highly able children, e.g. 'traditional Maori methods of education, where children who displayed ability and interest in a particular field were often taken under the wing of a tohunga or expert and given private tuition' (Taylor 1996, p. 401).

While a common cultural identity may add an extra dimension of empathy to a mentoring relationship, it is not always essential, so long as the mentor is sensitive to and respectful of the culture of his or her 'apprentice'. The crucial thing is their shared passion for an activity or domain of learning. Delisle (1999) observes that:

> Mentor relationships tend to be especially effective with young gifted women seeking same-sex role models to emulate in career direction and selection (Kaufmann *et al.* 1986), as well as for economically disadvantaged gifted youth, who may need the opportunity to see possibilities that exist outside of the limited domain of their neighborhoods. (Olszewski-Kubilius and Scott 1993, p. 242)

At Meriden, a private girls' school in Sydney, gifted students were matched with community mentors who assisted them in conducting an individual investigation of a self-chosen issue (Christie 1995). The adult mentor provided advice on the research processes used by the students as well as being a role model for success in the area of each student's special interest. Several of the projects undertaken by the gifted students had affective, often therapeutic, aspects relating to the girls' own lives. For example, one seventh grade girl who was agoraphobic chose to investigate 'Animal behaviour and the effectiveness of psychotherapy for animals', thus dealing vicariously with her own concerns. Another seventh grade student, who focused her investigation on 'play therapy', had an intellectually impaired younger sister, so had an emotional reason for her choice of topic too. For culturally diverse students the self-chosen investigation may relate to their cultural identity, perhaps in response to what Modood (1992, pp. 6 and 65) terms 'cultural-racism'. Matthews (1999, pp. 6 and 66) recommends that gifted students be encouraged to choose social-emotional issues as the content for independent study projects they undertake as part of a differentiation curriculum, as a means to the end of greater awareness of self and others (including the culturally diverse).

Computer technology
While computer technology and Internet access provide enrichment and extension opportunities for all gifted students, they may be particularly effective in overcoming some of the difficulties faced by culturally diverse gifted students:

- Perhaps the greatest advantage for gifted students is that it allows them access to ideas and information on the basis of readiness and interest, rather than some preconception about what they are capable of. A significant benefit of online provision is the relative anonymity of participation where gifted students are judged on their responses and contributions rather than age, gender, appearance or culture. Internet or e-mail communication enables even the most reserved or shy student to contribute to a discussion, without interruption, and to have his or her ideas considered by the other members of the class. As Kelly (1998) says of the online courses she manages: 'What we lose in spontaneity we gain in depth. A child has more spontaneous interaction in their "real" school and at home, with more emphasis on reflective discussion with us' (p. 25). Thus, a student who may be reluctant to participate actively in a classroom discussion or task – for fear of peer rejection or of personal inadequacy – may feel more comfortable about doing so online.

- A corollary of the previous point is that students with similar advanced skills or interests but from different schools, or even towns/cities, are able to form an online 'class' or extension group. Hence, an online class of high potential but under-achieving students, perhaps in a particular subject, could be formed to address their special needs. Such classes could be national, regional or local in composition and because of their nature there would be considerable flexibility in their duration and in who acts as teacher.

- Another virtue of online provision for the gifted is economy of scale, e.g. by having one adult act as mentor to a small group of like-minded students, rather than restricting mentoring to a one-to-one arrangement. Mentoring can be a highly effective means of encouraging gifted students to pursue areas of special interest, under the guidance of an adult whose expertise in that area is extensive, but finding sufficient mentors who are able to give up time from their already busy professional lives can be difficult, especially in smaller or relatively isolated communities. Mentoring of a group has been shown to work effectively using fax and traditional mail, where networks of up to 25 talented young astronomers, cartoonists, and writers, led by single mentors, were run over periods of one to two years (Bailey 1995) and already there have been successful trials of small group mentoring of gifted students via e-mail (e.g. two mentoring networks serving groups of five students each) within the Tamworth District, another Australian rural school district (Burnett 1998).

- A further advantage of online learning is the convenience of fitting in the learning around other commitments, particularly as access becomes more readily available through home and community outlets. Computer technology allows for flexibility in the time and place of participation – at home as well as, or instead of, at school; on weekends as well as during the school week; and at times that fit in with the students' sporting, cultural or family work commitments.

- In an age when 'virtual universities' are already in existence and likely to become major alternatives to traditional tertiary access, there would seem to be a significant advantage in culturally different gifted students gaining early experience of distance education by this means, to encourage and facilitate their subsequent enrolment in online university courses or other forms of post-compulsory-schooling online learning. The opportunity for gifted students to undertake tertiary study while remaining within the family and community support structure may afford them social-emotional as well as financial relief. Furthermore, the possibility of dual enrolment in secondary school and university may be facilitated as tertiary courses increasingly become available via online teaching.

Other considerations
Butler-Por (1994) reported promising outcomes from a programme in Israel for under-achieving culturally different children who were gifted. One component of the programme involved 28 eighth grade gifted students tutoring 28 fifth grade 'differently cultured gifted under-achievers' in the pursuit of personal projects chosen by the latter, as well as their jointly planning and implementing 'group activities aimed to involve the participants ... in contributing to the school and their community' (p. 219), to develop social responsibility. This cross-age tutoring led to improved motivation and participation by the culturally different students and to better understanding of these students and the difficulties they faced by the older students who were acting as their tutors. One of the best ways of reducing stereotyping is to allow direct personal experience to show the inadequacy of such superficial views, for example, to enable students to get to know each other as individuals, who are different in some ways but similar in many others. This is in harmony with Hulmes' (1998) conclusion that an important long-term goal of schooling is to enable students:

> to become more self-consciously aware of the beliefs which unite them and the differences which threaten good relationships between them. This may always have been the case in schools, but it is never more important than today, when the existence of cultural diversity among the members of a school community may be far greater than ever before. (p. 160)

Klein (1993) advocates the use of Lipman's 'Philosophy for Children' approach, not only because of its potential for improving thinking and reading skills but also for its social skill component and the principle that 'every student is being taken seriously ... it is safe to share your innermost feelings, values and aspirations' (p. 134). 'Philosophy for Children' involves the establishment of a 'community of inquiry' where ideas may be rejected, if found wanting under the scrutiny of critical analysis, but the person proffering them is not. Even if not implementing formally the 'Philosophy for Children' programme a teacher may adopt the values and attitudes underlying it, to promote a tolerant and accepting classroom environment. These include questioning the idea rather than the person, respecting the contributions of all class members, accepting that there may be more than one 'good' (or 'right') answer/solution to a question or problem, and recognising that all wisdom and knowledge does not reside with the teacher.

Another approach that should assist in both empathy building and personal self-awareness is de Bono's (1992) 'six thinking hats' strategy. Each 'hat' represents a way of thinking, with the red hat specifically legitimising the statement of feelings (without need of explanation or justification) but the blue hat making explicit the underlying assumption of this approach, that we always have choices about how we think. One of the strengths of the six thinking hats strategy is that it also focuses attention upon the content of any discussion or argument, rather than on the individuals involved, and it proves a structure for less dominant or confident students to challenge the views of peers (or of adults). In addition, it encourages students to consider more than one side of an issue, so that prejudice, preconceptions, tunnel vision or 'group think' are able to be challenged in a relatively unthreatening way.

There is evidence that African-American students are more likely (than Caucasian American students) to be 'relational, social, holistic, global learners' (Matthews 1999, p. 60). If similar learning style preferences are to be found in other cultural groups then one step toward addressing their social-emotional needs in school will be the recognition of this in the processes by which content is presented and assessed by teachers. Over the past decade Gardner's (1993) theory of multiple intelligences has become widely discussed and sometimes enthusiastically embraced by teachers for its recognition that the social-emotional areas of potential talent should be accorded the recognition they deserve. Noteworthy, then, is Bevan-Brown's (1996) advice that:

> When working with Maori children teachers must be mindful of the great importance placed on affective, interpersonal and intrapersonal qualities. They should identify children who are outstanding in these areas, encourage and reinforce these qualities whenever and wherever possible and provide opportunities where they can be manifest and nurtured. It is suggested that such an approach would benefit all children, regardless of ethnicity or ability. (p. 96)

Gibson's (1997) research in Australia also noted the significance of the 'personal intelligences' for the urban Aboriginal people she surveyed, highlighting the need for this ability domain to be recognised in formal identification processes and then in the forms of extension or enrichment provided.

The critical shift towards a multi-ethnic curriculum (and, therefore, a whole-school focus) is well-illustrated in Britain by the case of Prospect School in Berkshire. Formed in 1985 from the merger of two academically-successful, single-sex secondary schools, Prospect School recognised that a realignment in staff attitudes towards ethnic diversity would be necessary for long-term institutional change. A three-year Department of Education and Science-initiated project in Years Seven to Nine, which focused on greater multi-ethnicity in departmental syllabuses, resulted in more positive attitudes towards school by both black and white pupils, lessening of racial tension (nearly one-fifth had an ethnic minority background), raising of staff awareness and evidence of continued curriculum change (Elliott and Coleman 1994, p. 6).

Alternative forms of identification

A crucial first step toward achieving an optimal classroom environment for the identification of emotional well-being of gifted children from diverse cultures is the rejection by teachers of a deficit-based view of these children. Frasier (1993, p. 690) advocates adopting a more positive, proficiency-orientated view that focuses on their strengths and the support structures they have available in their school and community environments.

Being gifted but not recognised as such can be very frustrating for a child. Some gifted children who are recent immigrants may find initially that their capabilities are masked by their limited proficiency in English, as well as by their unfamiliarity with the practices of schools in their new country. This is why culturally diverse students may underperform on standardised tests and why other identification methods are needed to complement information derived from test scores. Frasier's F-TAP is a form of checklist that provides teachers or others with a set of research-based indicators to look for when seeking to identify high potential in students from different cultural backgrounds. Its underlying assumptions include that identification should focus upon dynamic rather than static evidence of high potential and that a 'profile, rather than cut off scores or weighting systems, provides the most effective and efficient way to display data for interpretation from test and non test sources' (Davis and Rimm 1998, p. 261). One English Local Education Authority Support Service issues the following guidance to help teachers recognise gifted pupils who have English as an additional language:

- pupils interpret the demands of tasks quickly using context clues, visual clues, examples set by peers, adult/peer gesture, etc;
- pupils demonstrate a keen ability to recognise routines, learn routines and anticipate routine events associated with the school day;
- pupils quickly absorb and are able to respond to everyday classroom instructions without depending on the example set by peers for a long period of time;
- pupils possess good visual and spatial skills which may be reflected in their representational drawing;
- pupils demonstrate good manual dexterity, particularly when engaged in pattern work and constructional activities;

- pupils in the early stages of speaking ask questions as well as respond to questions;
- pupils master a basic sight vocabulary quickly and show good memory recall of a number of language items when stories have been read to them.

Promising research into other forms of dynamic assessment has been conducted (Frasier 1993) and is currently under way at the University of New England, in Australia. This involves measuring students' capacity to improve when provided with structured guidance aimed at developing their metacognitive skills and feelings of self-efficacy.

Another dynamic form of identification is what has been termed 'identification by provision', whereby a wide range of students is given access to high-interest, high-challenge activities (of the kind sometimes reserved for the 'identified gifted') and their responses analysed for signs of previously hidden potential. Those whose responses are most promising may then be given further opportunities – perhaps including psychometric testing but certainly involving enrichment or extension provisions – to confirm and develop their high potential.

According to Torrance (1998), a compelling reason for encouraging young (i.e. up to grade three) children from cultural minorities to express their emotional capacities is that this will enable an insightful observer to identify high learning potential that may otherwise remain dormant. He lists a set of indicators that he terms 'creative positives' which his observations suggest occur 'with a rather high degree of frequency' (p. 96) in culturally different children. While 'emotional responsiveness' is the 17th item in his list, it is apparent that a strong affective theme runs through all items, these being:

1. Ability to express feelings and emotions.
2. Ability to improvise with commonplace materials and objects.
3. Articulateness in role playing, sociodrama and story telling.
4. Enjoyment of and ability in visual arts, such as drawing, painting and sculpture.
5. Enjoyment of and ability in creative movement, dance, dramatics, and so forth.
6. Enjoyment of and ability in music, rhythm and so forth.
7. Use of expressive speech.
8. Fluency and flexibility in figural media.
9. Enjoyment of and skills in group activities, problem solving, and so forth.
10. Responsiveness to the concrete.
11. Responsiveness to the kinesthetic.
12. Expressiveness of gestures, body language and so forth, and ability to interpret body language.
13. Humor.
14. Richess of imagery in informal language.

15. Originality of ideas in problem solving.
16. Problem centredness or persistence in problem solving.
17. Emotional responsiveness (Torrance 1998, p. 97).

In discussing each of these in detail, Torrance (1998) comments that:

> Unless students are provided learning experiences in which they can manifest their giftedness in expressing feelings and emotions, this type of giftedness is not likely to be discovered …

> Because there is a general lack of objective indicators of emotional expression, one is not likely to find much evidence in scientific research for this talent as a strength of culturally different groups. I can only say that this is one of the most frequently observed of the creative positives when my students record their observations of culturally different and poor children in our summer workshops, and that emotional expression has characterized and continues to characterize the artistic performances of the culturally different. (p. 98)

Just as a trial period is recommended for all instances of acceleration, so it has been suggested (Delisle 1992, p. 184) that culturally diverse students be allowed trial participation in special provisions for the gifted, not just as a way of assessing their readiness but also to encourage them to experience activities that they may otherwise shun, through fear of inadequacy or concern about peer rejection. Explaining the value of these opportunities would be another useful role for home–school liaison officers to adopt.

While identification is not a corridor of receding mirrors, it remains wise to see it as a never-ending process, though mainly with a diagnostic purpose rather than a labelling one. That is, it becomes part of the on-going teaching process, rather than being seen as a task that must be completed before any form of provision is attempted. This is especially crucial for potentially gifted students from culturally different backgrounds.

Conclusion

It is important for teachers to tap the insights of parents and other members of the wider community with culturally specific knowledge if the identification process is to be more inclusive and fair, as well as to understand better the social-emotional needs of all gifted children. Furthermore, Tomlinson *et al.* (1997) report that identifying potential talent in culturally diverse students can have a positive effect on the self-esteem of their parents, as well as on that of the students themselves. For example, one parent of a student in Project START (Support To Affirm Rising Talent) commented, 'The school thinks my kid is smart. That must mean I'm okay too – that I'm doing something right' (p. 12). The creation of a positive self-fulfilling prophecy for high-potential but under-achieving students from diverse cultures requires a combination of realistic expectations, more culturally fair and appropriate identification methods, and forms of provision that respect cultural as well as individual differences.

In their conclusions about the effectiveness of Project START Tomlinson *et al.* (1997) provide an overview that could serve as the ideal toward which all provision for culturally diverse students is aimed, namely:

> When a teacher begins to think about a child in more positive than negative ways, when a classroom becomes more flexible, when a parent hears a message from a school that a child is worth special investment, when the doors to school seem open and inviting, when someone from outside the school comes and spends time with a child, important transformations occur. Teachers emphasise what is right with a child rather than what is wrong. (p. 17)

Having teachers appreciate that high academic or creative potential does occur in culturally diverse students – even if the signs of this are often less obvious than in the case of those students who are 'teacher pleasers' – is the necessary first step on the path to ensuring that equity and excellence co-exist. Then the challenge is to ensure that more accurate and inclusive identification is followed by programmes and provisions likely to support and nurture this potential into confident achievement that leads to personal fulfilment and raised aspirations for the future within and beyond school.

References

Adderholdt-Elliott, M. and Eller, S. H. (1989) 'Counselling students who are gifted through bibliotherapy', *Teaching Exceptional Children* 22(1), 26–31.

Bailey, S. (1995) 'Networking: birds of a feather work together', *Gifted* 92, 19–23.

Bailey, S. and Chaffey, G. (1998) 'Talent development in Aboriginal students: two projects in north west New South Wales', *TalentEd* 16(4), 1–5.

Bevan-Brown, J. (1996) 'Special abilities: a Maori perspective', in McAlpine, D. and Moltzen, R. (eds) *Gifted and Talented: New Zealand Perspectives*. Palmerston North, NZ: ERDC Press.

Betts, G. T. (1986) 'The autonomous learner model for the gifted and talented', in Renzulli, J. S. (ed.) *Systems and Models for Developing Programs for the Gifted and Talented*. Mansfield Center: Creative Learning Press.

Burnett, B. (1998) *NetMentor Trial Report: Tamworth District*. Unpublished report.

Butler-Por, N. (1994) 'Gifted differently cultured underachievers in Israel', in Heller, K. A. and Hany, E. A. (eds) *Competence and Responsibility: The Third European Conference of the European Council for High Ability held in Munich (Germany) October 11-14, Vol. 2, Proceedings of the Conference.* Göttingen: Hogrefe and Huber.

Christie, W. (1995) 'Let their minds stretch', *TalentEd* 48, 7–14.

Davis, G. A. and Rimm, S. B. (1998) *Education of the Gifted and Talented.* Boston: Allyn and Bacon.

Day, A. (1992) 'Aboriginal students succeeding in the senior high school years: a strengthening and changing Aboriginality challenges the negative stereotype', *The Australasian Journal of Gifted Education* 1(2), 14–26.

de Bono, E. (1992) *Six Thinking Hats for Schools.* Melbourne: Hawker Brownlow Education.

Delisle, J. R. (1992) *Guiding the Social and Emotional Development of Gifted Youth.* New York: Longman.

Delisle, J. R. (1999) *Once Upon a Mind: The Stories and Scholars of Gifted Child Education.* Fort Worth, TX: Harcourt Brace College Publishers.

Duffy, B. (1998) *Supporting Creativity and Imagination in the Early Years.* Buckingham: Open University Press.

Elliott, G. and Coleman, C. (1994) 'Towards a curriculum for ethnic diversity', *TOPIC* 11(7), 1–6.

Ford, D. Y. (1995) *Counselling Gifted African American Students: Promoting Achievement, Identity and Social and Emotional Well Being.* Storrs, CT: The National Research Centre on the Gifted and Talented.

Ford, D. Y. (1996) *Reversing Underachievement Among Gifted Black Students: Promising Practices and Programs.* New York: Teachers College Press.

Frasier, M. M. (1993) 'Issues, problems and programs in nurturing the disadvantaged and culturally different talented', in Heller, K. A., Mönks, F. J. and Passow, A. H. (eds) *International Handbook of Research and Development of Giftedness and Talent.* Oxford: Pergamon.

Frasier, M. M., Garcia, J. H. and Passow, A. H. (1995) *A Review of Assessment Issues in Gifted Education and their Implications for Identifying Gifted Minority Students.* Storrs, CT: The National Research Center on the Gifted and Talented.

Gardner, H. (1993) *Frames of Mind: The Theory of Multiple Intelligences.* New York: Basic Books.

Gibson, K. (1997) 'Identifying issues', in Knight, B. A. and Bailey, S. (eds) *Parents as Lifelong Teachers of the Gifted.* Melbourne: Hawker Brownlow Education.

Gillborn, D. (1990) *Race, Ethnicity and Education.* London: Unwin and Hyman.

Goleman, D. (1996) *Emotional Intelligence.* London: Bloomsbury.

Gross, M. U. M. (1989) 'The pursuit of excellence or the search for intimacy? The forced-choice dilemma of gifted youth', *Roeper Review* 11(4), 189–93.

Hulmes, E. (1989) *Education and Cultural Diversity*. London: Longman.

Kelly, L. (1998) 'Information technology and the education of the gifted', *Gifted* **105**(1), 24–7.

Klein, G. (1993) *Education Towards Race Equality*. London: Cassell.

Maker, C. J. and Schiever, S. W. (eds) (1989) *Critical Issues in Gifted Education, Volume II: Defensible Programs for Cultural and Ethnic Minorities*. Austin, TX: Pro-Ed.

Matthews, D. J. (1999) 'Enhancing learning outcomes for diversely gifted adolescents: education in the social/emotional domain', *Journal of Secondary Gifted Education* **10**(2), 57–68.

Modood, T. (1992) *Not Easy Being British: Colour, Culture and Citizenship*. Stoke-on-Trent: Runnymede Trust and Trentham Books.

Novick, R. (1998) 'The comfort corner: fostering resiliency and emotional intelligence', *Childhood Education* **74**(4), 200–4.

Plummer, D. L. (1995) 'Serving the needs of gifted children from a multi-cultural perspective', in Genshaft, J. L., Bireley, M. and Hollinger, C. L. (eds) *Serving Gifted and Talented Students: A Resource for School Personnel*. Austin, TX: Pro-Ed.

Rawlinson, C. (1996) 'Self-concept, self-efficacy and program enrichment', in McAlpine, D. and Moltzen, R. (eds) *Gifted and Talented: New Zealand Perspectives*. Palmerston North, NZ: ERDC Press.

Taylor, S. (1996) 'Social and emotional development', in McAlpine, D. and Moltzen, R. (eds) *Gifted and Talented: New Zealand Perspectives*. Palmerston North, NZ: ERDC Press.

Tomlinson, C. A., Callaghan, C. M. and Lelli, K. M. (1997) 'Challenging expectations: case studies of high potential, culturally diverse young children', *Gifted Children Quarterly* **41**(2), 5–17.

Torrance, E. P. (1998) 'Talent among children who are economically disadvantaged or culturally different', in Smutny, J. F. (ed.) *The Young Gifted Child: Potential and Promise, an Anthology*. Cresskill, NJ: Hampton Press.

VanTassel-Baska, J., Olszewski-Kubilius, P. and Kulieke, M. (1994) 'A study of self-concept and social support in advantaged and disadvantaged seventh and eighth grade gifted students', *Roeper Review* **16**(3), 186–91.

CHAPTER 7

Able and talented learners from socio-economically disadvantaged communities

Belle Wallace

A humanising and enriching education for all learners

Before the particular needs of able and talented pupils who are perceived as 'socially or economically disadvantaged' can be discussed, it is necessary to paint a number of canvasses against which major issues of concern can be highlighted. With this in mind, this chapter begins by examining a number of theoretical and philosophical stances which the author perceives as important with regard to the education of all learners.

In any discussion of the needs of able learners we must affirm that all learners' needs must be subsumed within the broad concept of what constitutes a humanising curriculum for all learners and teachers. This affirmation immediately dispels the idea that able learners need 'special' or 'preferential' treatment as compared with other children. There is no better way to describe a 'humanising' curriculum than to echo and extend the words of Carl Rogers (1983).

A humanising curriculum seeks to provide and support:

- a climate of trust in the classroom in which curiosity and the natural desire to learn is nourished and enhanced;
- a participatory mode of decision-making in aspects of learning in which pupils, teachers and administrators play a part;
- a learning situation which helps pupils to prize themselves, building their confidence and self-esteem;
- a sense of excitement in emotional and intellectual discovery which leads pupils and teachers to become lifelong learners;

- an environment in which teachers are enabled to develop the attitudes and skills which research has shown to be effective in facilitating learning; and
- an enhancement of teachers' self-esteem as caring professionals.

The above characteristics of a humanising education assume that the school curriculum is relevant to the needs of the pupils: that learning needs are negotiated between learner, parent and teacher and supported by the school administrators; that attention is given to the affective needs of the learners, both on an individual level and on a social level; that teachers have the opportunity for ongoing development of their skills and understanding and that they are valued and supported in what is a very demanding profession. However, and most importantly, these characteristics of a humanising education are not the responsibility of teachers as a single group of individuals: they are developed through complex interactions between governmental demands and expectations; the demands of business and commerce; the school and its values and goals; the parents with their expectations and support; the peer group with its norms and interests; the community through the collective opportunities it provides and, of course, the children themselves with their individual personalities and abilities. Often the interests and goals of all these factors collide and contradict each other and, hence, the materialisation of the concept of a humanising curriculum into day-to-day practice can be compared to the merging of rivers into a turbulent sea.

Butler-Por (1987) complements and extends the idea of a humanising curriculum in her analysis of the prerequisite needs for 'joy in learning'. She proposes a number of essential social-emotional and motivational factors that every child should experience at home and at school in order to develop and sustain a constructive attitude towards school learning. This assumes, of course, that school learning is derived from ethical, justifiable and desirable goals. The prerequisites for 'joy in learning' include:

- social and emotional factors: trust in the self and in others, autonomy, initiative and self-confidence; and
- motivational factors: curiosity, respect for individual differences, mastery and competence learning, challenge and stimulus, encouragement of unconventional modes of learning, and parents' and teachers' support.

In this analysis, Butler-Por emphasises the affective needs of the child. I would additionally stress that parents and teachers also have essential affective needs if they are to have the skills and energy to provide what children in their care and under their influence need for sustained growth.

However, even a humanising and enriching curriculum for all children has enmeshed within it an amalgam of differing individual abilities and personalities, strengths and weaknesses, interests and experiences. When we are specifically considering the needs of very able learners, we have to think along a number of dimensions.

An extended concept of 'able' and 'talented' within a humanising and enriching curriculum

When we are discussing the needs of very able learners, even within an enriching and humanising curriculum, we can only say that their current level of functioning can often lead to exceptional adult accomplishment but not always. We can only talk about potential that needs to be nurtured at that time because the children demonstrate an obvious need. Therefore, for the remainder of this chapter, when we discuss various issues, we will regard references to any child's current manifestation of high ability or talent only as an indication of possible future performance. Feuerstein and Tannenbaum (1993) discuss factors that impinge on the flowering of exceptional performances and products:

> Obviously, what accounts for failure to realise high potential is either an absence or contamination of factors responsible for success. The exact nature of these elements is still largely a mystery, but whatever they are, it is possible to separate them into five strands that form a complex, elegant filigree to produce giftedness. The strands that contribute to the mesh include: (a) High General Ability, defined as superior abstract reasoning skills, utilised in finding and solving complex problems in many domains of productivity and performance; (b) Special Aptitudes, applied exclusively to problems that are domain specific; (c) Non-intellective Facilitators, of brilliant performance, including drive, dedication, good work habits, willingness to take creative risks, and other personal idiosyncrasies; (d) Environmental Support Systems, anchored mainly in the family, the school and the peer group, which supply the necessary education, encouragement and opportunities to excel; and (e) Chance or Luck, such as meeting the right people who have the right connections, and being within earshot when opportunity knocks. (p. 12)

Renzulli (in Renzulli and Reis 1986) emphasises that gifted behaviours can be *developed* and that there are factors other than high IQ which contribute to outstanding performance. He argues against 'tidy' and 'comfortable' notions of definition and identification and labels of 'gifted' or 'not gifted'. Instead he argues that our identification of learners with high potential must accept that certain students (not all students), at certain times (not all the time), will show high level abilities if they are presented with appropriate opportunities.

Now that the background canvas has been painted we can begin to highlight issues against this in order to consider the needs of potentially able and talented children who come from socially and economically disadvantaged backgrounds.

An examination of some of the factors in socio-economically disadvantaged communities which inhibit the development of high level abilities and talents

There are four obvious major categories of influence on the behaviour of any individual. These are: the family, the school, the peer group and the community. In addition, we must always bear in mind that every person has a compilation of traits and personal characteristics which are derived from genetic and innate factors, and these traits, together with factors in the environment, constellate into the unique individual. In this chapter we will examine the influence of the family and the school in low socio-economic areas, although both these influences impinge on each other, and we will draw in factors regarding the peer group and the community which are enmeshed in both.

The family

The importance of language development on the development of ability
It is universally accepted that the development of a child's capacity to do well is heavily reliant on the support and encouragement of the parents. This has been well documented by writers such as Whitmore (1979), Passow (1982), Baldwin (1985), Bloom (1985), Davis and Rimm (1985), Rimm (1990) and Freeman (1991), and a number of important issues emerge from their collective writing.

Perhaps the most important issue lies in the domain of language development, since all children use language to analyse and generalise meaning and to build up a repertoire of knowledge and ideas that form the basic scaffolding for more complex learning. Children from all cultures and strata of society have language but Cummins (1983) argues that learners are empowered or disabled by the degree to which:

- pupils' native or home language is incorporated into school language;
- learners' community values are incorporated into school activities;
- teaching first promotes and then extends the active use of the learner's language; and
- pupils' cultural strengths are recognised and fostered.

In school learning pupils need a wide range of cognitive language tools that may not be within the normal repertoire of family discourse. Vygotsky (Foreman and Cazden 1985) discusses the vital role of mediation in language development by which language and thought develops through the social transactions of meaning which first occur in the family. These early interactions are powerfully pervasive and value laden and when early school experiences inculcate language and values that are different from the home then the learner begins at a very young age to feel alienated from school experiences. Freeman (1993) states:

Parents who have themselves been brought up in culturally impoverished circumstances may lack familiarity with easy verbal communication which affects their children's intellectual growth. Cultural disadvantage usually brings three main psychological handicaps in the areas of perception and attention, verbal and intellectual abilities and motivation. (p. 673)

Often in socio-economically disadvantaged homes both parents are consumed by the necessary task of earning a living doing low status work and there is little time, energy or motivation for reading stories, intensive and sustained conversation and mediated play. There is also little money for extended cultural activities that broaden life experiences and open up awareness of a wide range of interests and activities. When psychometric tests are used to test learners in low socio-economic areas the general tendency is for many low-achieving learners who are perceived as potentially able by their teachers to score highly on the non-verbal aspects of the tests and not so highly on the verbal aspects (Wallace 1983a). Obviously psychometric tests have limitations that are not discussed here but they do correlate highly with traditional school achievement that demands a high level of school, i.e. verbal language. Radford (1990) quoted in Freeman (1993, p. 672) found that exceptional early achievers, although appearing to come from homes of low socio-economic status, all came from homes which were 'lively, stimulating and often highly verbal'.

In order to empower all learners in the school situation, learning must be rooted in the home language which is then used as the scaffolding from which extended language is developed. And, of course, with articulate middle-class learners this is usually the case since school language and home language form a common matrix of meaning. However, while it can be argued that disadvantaged very able children are fast learners and with encouragement and support from sympathetic teachers can acquire school language and advanced cognitive language rapidly, when this happens a communication gulf rapidly develops between the child and the parents. This situation obviously needs careful counselling between the learner and the family if the learner and the family are to understand and cope with the situation. The following reconstructions from typical case studies illustrate this need very poignantly (Wallace 1983b):

I'm interested in world politics but I never talk to my parents about what I read in the newspapers [in the school library]. They wouldn't be interested and they wouldn't understand anyway. Dad only reads the racing news and would just think I was putting one over on him and I would get a clip behind the ear for being cocky and mum never reads any kind of newspaper.

There's no hope of me even thinking of going to university. My dad would never let me stay on in school and I can only read when he's not around because he thinks books are a waste of time. I can't even talk to him because his eyes are glued to the TV.

The importance of positive self-concept and internal locus of control in high achievers
Goleman (1996) argues very strongly that emotional intelligence is the necessary requisite for the efficient development of all other forms of intelligent and creative functioning of human beings. Salovey and Mayer (1990) extend the notion of emotional intelligence and suggest a number of elements which need to be nurtured, namely: understanding the self and personal feelings; knowing how to manage anxiety and irritability; marshalling energies to complete a task; recognising emotion in others and generating empathy; and developing social competence. The grounding for the development of these abilities rests within the quality and type of family interactions which essentially mediate and lay the foundation for the growth of emotional intelligence through the kind of discipline prevalent in the home: the respect given to the feelings of the child; the time taken to negotiate behaviour outcomes; and the extent to which the family engages in reflection on emotional issues. Referring back to the importance of the development of the mediation of language discussed above, when parents are overwhelmed by the debilitating demands of low income survival, it is rare that time and energy is available for discussion of emotional development with the children. Often parents have neither the experience of, nor the language for, such lengthy discourse and matters of discipline revolve around crisis management and are non-negotiable.

The concept of locus of control resides in the degree to which the self is perceived as autonomous and in control over life circumstances. Rotter (1966) explains locus of control as perceived relationships between actions and outcomes of behaviour. Children with a strong internal locus of control perceive themselves as responsible for the outcomes of their own actions: they feel capable of making their own decisions and are highly motivated to achieve, persistent and task committed. Children with a strong external locus of control perceive themselves as being manipulated by circumstances and hence powerless in a more powerful world.

Obviously parents who see themselves as autonomous decision-makers and who perceive themselves as having control over their lives are more likely to foster these abilities in their children. Studies such as Ausubel (1966) and Dweck and Elliot (1983) confirm that parents who encourage early independence and achievement related activities, rear children who tend to have an internal locus of control. It is not difficult to see that parents who themselves feel powerless in a society due to their poor social and economic circumstances rear children who feel powerless in a more powerful world. Many long-term studies such as Lefcourt (1983), Baldwin (1985) and Maker (1989), all indicate that learners from disadvantaged communities tend to have an external locus of control, feeling imprisoned by their home circumstances and experiences rather than empowered by them.

The development of positive self-concept is closely related to the development of internal locus of control and thus to what Bandura (1971, 1982) has called self-efficacy. Learners who feel good about themselves, who feel a sense of personal autonomy with control over their environment, are very likely to perceive and confirm through experience that their behaviour produces desired outcomes. Their motivation is high to persist in striving towards chosen goals. Styles of parenting can actively foster and encourage this behaviour, or unknowingly neglect or discourage the essential prerequisites for high level, goal-directed personal functioning.

The following reconstructions from typical case studies illustrate the dilemma of some young people locked into low socio-economic homes (Wallace 1983b):

I look after the children of a night because my mum works in the pub since my dad left and by the time they're in bed I'm too tired to do my homework. That's why I'm always in trouble with the teachers but there's nothing I can do about it. All I want to do is leave school and get a job.

Nobody does anything different in our street except work in the factory so I'll go there like all my friends. It's useless me thinking of doing anything different isn't it? In any case my parents haven't got the money to keep me in school.

The importance of fostering extended interests and activities in the home

In his retrospective study of highly talented achieving adults Bloom (1985) found that there was strong evidence that these individuals received sustained environmental support in the sense of motivational encouragement, supportive nurturance and breadth of experiences. Initially this was rooted in the family influences, values and interests that encouraged high achievement and stressed the importance of doing one's best. Bloom comments:

The parents' commitment to the productive use of time and doing one's best was evidenced in the values they taught their children. The parents expected all family members to learn this code of conduct, and the models the parents provided of working hard and setting high standards of performance were clearly recognized by the children. (p. 441)

… parents (or other family members), in pursuing their own interests, created situations that intrigued, interested, or involved the child … the child's interest was rewarded or encouraged, and the child did learn some simple skills … The parents encouraged the children's interest, provided opportunities for the children to learn in other ways as well … they provided resources and materials as well. (p. 448)

… the parents' interest and participation in the child's learning contributed significantly to his or her achievement in the field. We find it difficult to imagine how these children could have gotten [sic] good teachers, learned to practice regularly and thoroughly, and developed a value of and commitment to achievement in the talent field without a great deal of parental guidance and support. The role of the home in supporting the long process of talent development is only one piece of the picture but it is a crucial one. (p. 476)

In low socio-economic families, when money for essential survival is minimal, there is very little money available for visits to museums or theatres, for lessons in music or dance, for an extra television for private choice viewing, for cultural holidays, for school trips. In these circumstances, a child's range of enrichment and extension activities is narrow and confined to finding opportunities that are free and locally available. The child must rely on free community facilities and opportunities provided by the school.

Typical case study reconstructions highlight the problems of young learners who are under-stimulated at home:

In the holidays we just roam the streets because there's nothing else to do. Sometimes when we're larking around people think we're up to no good but we're just having a laugh;

and similarly:

A gang of us meet on the corner every night because the television is always on at home and we're not interested in the programmes our parents watch. (Wallace 1983b)

It is not difficult to imagine the escalation of youthful energy into acts that are anti-social and lead to trouble that intensifies into petty crime. However, some children do find escape routes either owing to their own initiative or to the encouragement of parents. These youngsters seem to have an ego strength that keeps them resilient, despite a potentially crippling environment, or there is a significant adult who provides support and encouragement:

My mum has always taken us to the library since we were little and now the librarian saves new books for us if she thinks we will be interested. Everyone in our family reads and sometimes there are over 20 books lying around.

I've always collected old bikes from scrap yards or people's gardens. I pay for them from the money I get from my paper round. Then I build and do up bikes like new and sell them. I've made a lot of money doing that.

Lots of people have old televisions and I take them off their hands. I've got a big collection and my dad has converted the loft for me to have a workshop and I spend all my spare time up there. (Wallace 1983b)

The school

The problems deriving from the families of able children from disadvantaged socio-economic backgrounds are obviously carried over into school. The difference in language between the home and school; the variance in values and attitudes; the possible lack of positive self-concept; an external locus of control; a lack of reinforced self-efficacy; and the difference in the background experiences of the children as compared with more affluent families, all impact on the school environment and the interaction between learner and teacher.

A summary of these traits is embedded in many compilations of the common characteristics of disadvantaged learners in the school context. One such compilation can be drawn from the long-term research conducted independently by educators such as Whitmore (1979), Baldwin (1985) and Rimm (1990). They draw attention to the following traits:

The learner demonstrates –

- an external locus of control and is unable to give attention to a task without supervision since the home background has provided the experience of obeying instructions and 'doing as s/he is told';
- a reliance on the support of the peer group with conformity to peer group expectations, since the peer group has been a focus for personal identity;
- a strong survival instinct with regard to physical hardships and a lack of experience of 'beauty' in life, since the environment has focused on necessities;
- practical problem-solving behaviour deriving from the need to survive on a day-to-day basis;
- everyday language rich in humour which laughs at people and their problems;
- awareness of social problems within the community with a sensitivity to everyday issues of fairness; and
- development of 'physical' toughness and appreciation of physical accomplishments.

It is important to state at the outset that the school cannot completely replace the family as the most important influence in the development of children but a school can work towards alleviating disadvantages in learners' lives. A school can aim to provide curriculum experiences that begin with learners' experiences and then consciously work to enrich and extend these experiences. A school can provide counselling and guidance to children and their families, can bring parents into dialogue with the school and its aims, and can involve the learners in aspects of decision-making. But all this involves a great deal of extra work and a heavy time and energy commitment on the part of teachers and this effort must have adequate funding and support.

Teacher recognition of potentially high achievers in low socio-economic areas
Wallace, working in the field of counselling and then in the field of provision for

able pupils (Essex (UK) 1963–83), found that teachers working in low socio-economic areas were generally reluctant and often unable to identify pupils with high-level ability. On the whole, teachers did not expect to find able children who came from poor homes and 'working class' areas. (This tendency has been confirmed by the findings of Butler-Por 1987, Sisk 1988 and Maker 1989.) Subsequently, Wallace compiled checklists of characteristics from 200 profiles of under-achievers who had been referred by teachers for educational psychological assessments. The test used diagnostically was the Wechsler Scale of Intelligence for Children and the general test findings indicated that the majority of pupils in the sample of 200 demonstrated a much higher than average non-verbal ability with considerably lower verbal ability. (See also Whitmore 1979, Baldwin 1985 and Rimm 1990.) However, the reports of the teachers and the educational psychologists provided a richer source of behavioural information about pupils with potential who were under-achieving. The list of characteristics that emerged is as follows:

The under-achiever may be:

- anti-school and critical of its values; often scathing in remarks about teachers and lacking in enthusiasm for most school subjects;
- frequently and abrasively humorous with an ironic perception of other people's weaknesses;
- orally good while written work is poor and incomplete; not interested in seeking the teacher's approval by completing work;
- apparently bored and lethargic, lacking energy and motivation; watches the time and is anxious to finish the day and leave school;
- restless, inattentive and easily distracted, often at the root of mischief and jokes;
- absorbed in a private world, often wasting time by doing nothing or distracting other pupils;
- friendly with older pupils, deliberately seeking their company and often accepted by them;
- impatient and critical, sometimes rude and insolent, finding difficulty in making relations with peers and teachers;
- inclined to be emotionally unstable, very prone to moodiness and bad temper, apparently easily frustrated and lacking in kindliness towards others;
- outwardly self-sufficient and apparently careless or indifferent to school standards;
- irregular in attendance but able to keep up with the other children;
- defensive but very astute in argument and self-justification;
- often the leader of the malcontents and the anti-school group;
- well endowed with 'low cunning' and survival skills; and
- able to manipulate others while not being personally committed or involved. (Wallace 1983a, pp. 39–40)

During this period, Essex was committed to providing residential courses for groups of able pupils and to promoting school-based curriculum enrichment and extension programmes (see also Chapter 3). As a result of in-service courses to develop teachers' awareness of the needs of high potential pupils, many teachers working in differing socio-economic areas voluntarily gave their time after school, over weekends and during the holidays to prepare and teach in curriculum enrichment and extension courses. On all courses, a great emphasis was placed on developing thinking and problem-solving skills, good inter-personal relations between pupils and teachers, providing extensive counselling opportunities, creating projects that were interesting and exciting, developing mentorships that would continue after the course. Some courses were for children from diverse backgrounds and others were especially for children from low socio-economic backgrounds. With the latter groups, the teachers, in evaluating the courses, collectively commented on the characteristics of the learners that emerged. The following list summarises their observations:

Under-achieving pupils when involved and motivated can be:

- interested, inventive and original although impatient and reluctant to persevere with in-between stages;
- quick to learn new concepts and able to pose problems and to solve them ingeniously, especially those unrelated to school tasks or 'academic' subjects;
- able to ask provocative, searching questions and very aware of problems about people and life generally;
- persevering when motivated, sometimes performing at a very high level in one or two areas only, and particularly when the relationship with the teacher is good;
- inventive in response to open-ended questions;
- philosophical and wise about everyday problems and commonsense issues; and
- perceptive in discussion about people's motives, needs and frailties. (Wallace 1983a, p. 40)

The pupils from low socio-economic areas also evaluated the courses and some of their comments are quoted below:

We could choose the project that interested us and I chose the one on modern art although I didn't know anything about it because I've never been to an art gallery. The teacher explained all these modern pictures and then we tried to explain some ourselves. I used my imagination and thought up some good ideas! Then we created our own modern art and had to explain it.

It was a break from school and I could concentrate on one thing for as long as I liked. The best bit was talking to other people and I made friends with someone who collects televisions like me. We are going to swap things with each other in the holidays.

The teachers were like friends and we could talk to them about anything we wanted. I was a mediaeval lord of the manor and we discussed how I would manage the peasants who worked on my land. If you were a peasant you had a very hard life and you couldn't make your own decisions. I sometimes feel that my life is like a modern peasant because I have no control over my life. (Wallace 1983b)

While the writer would strongly advocate a general policy of providing school-wide enrichment for all pupils, then providing curriculum extension for those pupils who demonstrate the need, the residential courses in Essex served a number of purposes. Firstly, teachers were able to concentrate their energy and attention with a single focus; they were able to experience what able pupils were capable of doing, especially those with a history of under-achievement. Secondly, pupils were able to work in-depth with other able peers and many long-term friendships were formed. Pupils with a history of under-achievement were given a chance to 'make a fresh start' unhampered by their school and peer group reputation; they were introduced to new areas of interest and often developed a mentoring relationship with teachers which continued after the courses.

Providing School-Wide Enrichment
Renzulli (in Renzulli and Reis 1986) outlines his rationale for the development of a programme of School-Wide Enrichment. He argues that the provision of enrichment activities for an identified few 'gifted' learners pre-supposes that this is both possible and desirable. He proposes the establishment of a School-Wide Enrichment Team that should organise an enrichment programme for the whole school, recruiting parents, community resource persons, administrators, teachers, art/music/sports specialists, librarians and media specialists as the key group of organisers. However, he stresses the importance of consultation and communication with all teachers and parents so that they feel a sense of ownership, are involved, and are able to contribute their ideas and offer their talents and time. Wallace (1983a) also argues for School-Wide Enrichment programmes so that all pupils have access to opportunities to discover what they are interested in and what they have talent for. This kind of provision not only allows the children to discover their strengths and talents but it also gives the teachers opportunities to discover children who have special attributes and unexpected talents.

There is not the space to give detail of Renzulli's extensive and well-developed programme here, only the main characteristics of his approach are outlined below.

Teachers in a school work collectively to develop:

1. assessments of learners' strengths including abilities, interests and learning styles;

2. curriculum compacting involving modification of the amount of time able learners spend on repetitive tasks so as to save time to spend on more advanced tasks;

3. the introduction of exploratory activities not usually included in the normal curriculum to increase awareness and widen interests;

4. training in group work that enhances learners' affective and cognitive skills, learning-how-to-learn skills, research and reference skills, and communication skills; and

5. individual and small group investigations of real problems.

In the light of the problems of disadvantaged learners which were highlighted in the earlier sections of this chapter, and in line with point (4) above, it is proposed to outline the basic principles underlying an intervention programme called TASC (Thinking Actively in a Social Context) which is specifically aimed at developing the cognitive and affective abilities of disadvantaged children from low socio-economic and culturally deprived backgrounds. The writers (Wallace and Adams 1993b) argue that the principles should underlie all curriculum development that is aimed at empowering learners. The background to the intervention programme has been described elsewhere (Adams 1985, 1986, 1988 and Wallace and Adams 1987, 1988, 1993a, 1993b). Only the major principles will be outlined here.

The basic theoretical rationale on which the TASC intervention programme is based

The fundamental premise that underlies TASC is that cognitive and affective skills can be taught and that all individuals are capable of improving their level of functioning given the appropriate learning experiences. This premise is supported by the work of Bandura (1971, 1982), Bandura and Walters (1963), Sternberg (1983, 1985a, 1985b, 1985c, 1986) and Vygotsky (1978).

Bandura suggests that a child's behaviour is modelled on the behaviour of significant others and the child needs to experience this model as positively reinforcing. The styles of discipline the child experiences influence the child's belief in the self as having some or no control over the environment. The acquisition of cognitive processes is influenced by: the child's perception of his or her degree of self-efficacy, i.e. the child is convinced that s/he can produce certain outcomes; and the child's belief that s/he can regulate her or his behaviour through self-observation, self-judgement and self-response, i.e. through metacognition. A positive sense of the self, together with an internal locus of control, are prerequisites for successful learning and task commitment. This makes self-direction through goal-setting and self-evaluation possible.

Sternberg posits the theory that intelligence is mental activity directed towards the purposeful adaptation to, and the selection and shaping of, real world environments relevant to one's life. Intelligence involves being able to deal effectively with novel situations and to automise relevant skills and that a repertoire of these skills can be successfully taught and automised thus increasing an individual's mental capacity. These skills reside in the acquisition of problem-solving skills and in the reflection on the efficacy of those skills, i.e. through metacognition.

Vygotsky (in Bruner 1984, 1985) emphasises that intellectual development is not just the acquiring of experience, it is the social transaction of meaning through the mediation of experience by adults, teachers and more capable peers. The tutor performs the task of providing 'scaffolding' for the learner who gradually becomes capable and independent. When this process is inadequate the learner fails to develop fully effective cognitive functions resulting in the depressed functioning of the individual, but this can be remedied by appropriate intervention.

A brief outline of the TASC principles and methodology

The broad outline of the TASC model is given in Figure 7.1. This model is intended as a guide for the development of a process of interactive teaching and learning which systematically develops thinking and problem-solving skills together with the appropriate language skills.

There is not the space within this chapter to explain the model in detail (see Wallace and Adams 1993b for a detailed explanation). However, a number of salient points are outlined below:

- The model takes into account the universal needs of all learners and is meant to be used as a framework for groups of teachers to develop their own programmes.
- The overall model for problem-solving and the selected tools for effective thinking were derived from an action research programme which involved close, reflective and pragmatic collaboration with teachers and pupils. In implementing the TASC model the processes of problem-solving must always be shared with the learners and should accommodate problems that are relevant to the particular group of learners.
- The fundamental teaching methodology focuses on giving attention to the motivational needs of the learner; giving positive feedback and building confidence in the self as a competent problem-solver.
- The progression of teaching is from modelling by the teacher, to guided activity by the learner, to eventually autonomous action by the learner. The teacher 'thinks aloud' the TASC processes of her/his thinking as a model for the pupils.

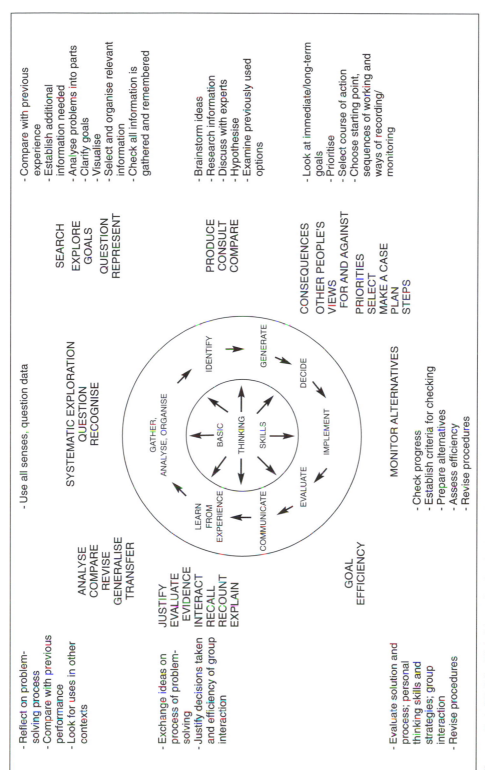

Figure 7.1 TASC: Thinking Actively in a Social Context. Detail of the problem-solving framework and selected tools for effective thinking

- The emphasis is on oral work in small groups to give greater time for communication and feedback between learners.
- At every stage, learners should be given time to engage in reflection on their thinking processes. Constant introspection and the verbalisation of progress and insights are essential if the learners are to become increasingly aware of their own thinking processes. Every effort must be made to transfer skills to other contexts.

Comment on recent national guidelines to improve pupil performance in low socio-economic areas

The Department for Education and Employment (DfEE) has issued a document *Excellence in Cities* (1999) relating initially to schools in six targeted large inner urban areas. The government manifesto reads thus:

To provide more effectively for the aptitudes and aspirations of individual pupils we will:

- radically expand and recast the specialist and beacon school programmes, with a special emphasis on the inner cities…;
- extend opportunities for gifted and talented children with special programmes for the highest performing five to ten per cent of pupils in each secondary school…;
- launch a new network of learning centres, in the inner cities, developing existing schools as centres of excellence…;
- encourage setting by schools to meet individual aptitudes and abilities;
- give a new emphasis to literacy and numeracy teaching and ensure better transition from primary to secondary school … expand the number of summer schools and after-school programmes; and
- introduce a scheme of low cost home computer lease for pupils and adults who face particular disadvantages.

We will launch an immediate programme to build on success, overcome barriers to effective learning and tackle failure. This will:

- strengthen school leadership, with new measures to recruit and train successful teachers and headteachers, and to strengthen school governing bodies…;
- turn around the weakest schools…;
- modernise LEAs, ensuring that each has an effective strategy for school improvement…;
- tackle disruption in schools more effectively by ensuring that every school has access to a learning support unit…; and

- provide a 'learning mentor' for every young person who needs one…. (DfEE 1999, pp. 2–3)

The above manifesto must be commended as the stated intent of a government wanting to improve education for socio-economically disadvantaged learners. However, there are a number of serious considerations that need to be raised.

In the light of the issues arising from within socio-economically disadvantaged families as discussed earlier, it is unreasonable to expect that schools and teachers can rectify all the disadvantages that apply to learners. It is vital that families are drawn fully into any scheme for community upliftment. Parents need to understand, share the burden, and work alongside and as hard as the teachers towards the goals of the school. Most importantly, enabling styles of parenting need to be nurtured at an early stage in a child's development. By the time learners are in secondary school, behaviour patterns are entrenched, peer groups strong and under-achievement a definite syndrome; and rectifying this situation requires that an enormous amount of time be spent in counselling and guidance for individuals and groups.

Considering the ethical concept of a humanising curriculum for all pupils (Rogers 1983), the need for 'joy in learning' for all pupils (Butler-Por 1987) and the extended concept of 'gifts and talents' (Gardner 1983); it is difficult to accept the DfEE's stated policy of selecting the top 'five to ten per cent' in inner city schools for special provision of enrichment and extension activities. How are the chosen few to be selected? Since under-achievement in disadvantaged areas is widespread and many learners have not had the opportunities to discover what their talents might be, it is not fair educational practice to deny the 90 to 95 per cent the chance of 'remediating' their under-achievement through an enriched curriculum for all. Then in Renzulli's (1986) terms, as learners demonstrate the need, they are provided with extension opportunities.

If schools are going to set their pupils and have an 'able set', where are the chronically under-achieving able pupils to be placed? How is the syndrome of under-achievement to be rectified and who will be responsible for bridging the inevitable gaps in learning? Coupled with this problem, there is the problem of learners' under-developed cognitive functions and the need to develop effective thinking and problem-solving skills. How will teachers and parents be trained and supported? Improving standards in schools is not just a matter of getting better examination results on a content-based syllabus, it is a matter of empowering learners with 'learning how to learn' skills across a relevant and meaningful curriculum.

It has been argued earlier that a positive sense of self, an internal locus of control and a sense of self-efficacy are all vital requisites for self-directed and successful learning. A lack of these essential traits stems from deep and tenacious family roots and developing new attitudes and new values takes time and needs support for both the individual and the family.

In conclusion, the new government directives are to be applauded but unless the deeper issues are also addressed, then an enormous amount of money and teacher energy will be wasted and an enormous amount of pupil talent will continue to be undeveloped. Disadvantage has social, economic, linguistic, affective and cognitive causes and consequences and all these aspects must be addressed in the pursuit of 'excellence'.

References

Adams, H. B. (1985) 'The teaching of general problem-solving strategies', in *Developing Cognitive Strategies in Young Children: Saaled Conference Proceedings.* RSA: University of Durban-Westville.

Adams, H. B. (1986) 'Teaching general problem-solving strategies in the classroom', *Gifted Education International* 4(2), 84–9.

Adams, H. B. (1988) 'Assessment and development of potential of high school pupils in the third world context of KwaZulu/Natal Part 3, *Gifted Education International* 5(3), 132–7.

Ausubel, D. (1966) 'The effect of cultural deprivation on learning patterns', in Webster, S. (ed.) *The Disadvantaged Learner.* San Francisco: Chandler.

Baldwin, A. Y. (1985) 'Programs for the gifted and talented: issues concerning minority populations', in Horowitz, F. D. and O'Brien, M. (eds) *The Gifted and Talented: Developmental Perspectives.* Washington DC: American Psychological Association.

Bandura, A. (1971) *Social Learning Theory.* Englewood Cliffs, NJ: Prentice Hall.

Bandura, A. (1982) 'Self-efficacy mechanism in human agency', *American Psychologist* 37, 122–47.

Bandura, A. and Walters, R. H. (1963) *Social Learning Theory and Personality Development.* Englewood Cliffs, NJ: Prentice Hall.

Bloom, B. S. (ed.) (1985) *Developing Talent in Young People.* New York: Ballantine Books.

Bruner, J. (1984) 'Vygotsky's zone of proximal development: the hidden agenda', in Rogoff, B. and Wertsch, J. V. (eds) *Children's Learning in the Zone of Proximal Development.* San Francisco: Jossey-Bass.

Bruner, J. (1985) 'Vygotsky: a historical and conceptual perspective', in Wertsch, J. V. (ed.) *Culture, Communication and Cognition: Vygotskian Perspectives.* New York: Cambridge University Press.

Butler-Por, N. (1987) *Underachievers in School.* London: John Wiley.

Cummins, J. (1983) *Heritage Language Education: A Literature Review*. Toronto: Ministry of Education.

Davis, G. A. and Rimm, S. B. (1985) *Education of the Gifted and Talented*. Englewood Cliffs, NJ: Prentice Hall.

DfEE (1999) *Excellence in Cities*. London: DfEE Publications.

Dweck, C. S. and Elliot, E. E. (1983) 'Achievement Motivation', in Mussen, P. H. and Hetherington, E. M. (eds) *Handbook of Child Psychology* Vol. 4, *Socialisation, Personality and Social Development*. New York: John Wiley.

Feuerstein, R. and Tannenbaum, A. J. (1993) 'Mediating the learning experiences of gifted underachievers', in Wallace, B. and Adams, H. B. (eds) *Worldwide Perspectives on the Gifted Disadvantaged*. London: AB Academic Publishers.

Foreman, E. A. and Cazden, C. B. (1985) 'Exploring Vygotskian perspectives in education', in Wertsch, J. V. (ed.) *Culture, Communication and Cognition: Vygotskian Perspectives*. New York: Cambridge University Press.

Freeman, J. (1991) *Gifted Children Growing Up*. London: Cassell.

Freeman, J. (1993) 'Parents and families in nurturing giftedness and talent', in Heller, K. A., Mönks, F. J. and Passow, A. H. (eds) *International Handbook of Research and Development of Giftedness and Talent*. Oxford: Pergamon Press.

Gardner, H. (1983) *Frames of Mind*. New York: Basic Books.

Goleman, D. (1996) *Emotional Intelligence*. London: Bloomsbury.

Lefcourt, H. M. (ed.) (1983) *Research with the Locus of Control Construct Development and Social Problems 2*. New York: Academic Press.

Maker, C. J. (1989) 'Program for gifted minority students: a synthesis of perspectives', in Maker, C. J. and Schiever S. W. (eds) *Critical Issues in Gifted Education 2*. Austin, TX: PRO-ED Inc.

Maker, C. J. and Schiever, S. W. (eds) (1989) *Critical Issues in Gifted Education 2*. Austin, TX: PRO-ED Inc.

Passow, A. H. (1982) 'The gifted disadvantaged: some reflections in identifying and educating the disadvantaged/talented', in *Selected Proceedings from the Fifth National Conference on Disadvantaged Gifted/Talented*. Los Angeles, CA: The National/State Leadership Training Institute on the Gifted and the Talented.

Radford, J. (1990) *Child Prodigies and Exceptionally Early Achievers*. London: Harvester Wheatsheaf.

Renzulli, J. S. (1986) 'The three-ring conception of giftedness: a developmental model for creative productivity', in Sternberg, R. J. and Davidson, J. (eds) *Conceptions of Giftedness*. New York: Cambridge University Press.

Renzulli, J. S. and Reis, S. M. (1986) 'The enrichment triad/revolving door model: a schoolwide plan for the development of creative productivity', in Renzulli, J. S. (ed.) *Systems and Models For Developing Programs For The Gifted And Talented*. Mansfield Center, CT: Creative Learning Press Inc.

Rimm, S. (1990) 'Underachievement and superachievement: flip sides of the same psychological coin', in Colangelo, N. and Davis, G. (eds) *Handbook of Gifted Education.* Boston: Allyn and Bacon.

Rogers, C. (1983) *Freedom to Learn.* London: Charles E. Merrill.

Rotter, J. B. (1966) 'Generalised expectancies for internal versus external control of reinforcement', *Psychological Monographs* **80**, 1–281.

Salovey, P. and Mayer, J. D. (1990) 'Emotional intelligence', *Imagination, Cognition and Personality* **9**, 185–211.

Sisk, D. (1988) 'Children at risk: the identification of the gifted among the minority', *Gifted Education International* **5**(3), 138–41.

Sternberg, R. J. (1983) 'Criteria for intelligence skills training', *Educational Researcher* **12**, 6–12.

Sternberg, R. J. (1985a) 'Teaching critical thinking part 1: are we making critical mistakes?', *Phi Delta Kappa* **67**, 194–8.

Sternberg, R. J. (1985b) 'Teaching critical thinking part 2: possible solutions', *Phi Delta Kappa* **67**, 277–89.

Sternberg, R. J. (1985c) *Beyond IQ: A Triarchic Theory of Human Intelligence.* New York: Cambridge University Press.

Sternberg, R. J. (1986) *Intelligence Applied: Understanding and Increasing your Intelligence Skills.* San Diego: Harcourt Brace, Jovanovich.

Vygotsky, L. S. (ed.) (1978) *Mind in Society: The Development of Higher Psychological Processes.* Cambridge, MA: Harvard University Press.

Wallace, B. (1983a) *Teaching the Very Able Child.* London: Ward Lock Educational.

Wallace, B. (1983b) Personal Counselling Records (unpublished).

Wallace, B. (1988) 'Curriculum enrichment for all pupils then curriculum extension', *Critical Arts: A Journal for Cultural Studies* **4**(1), 4–5.

Wallace, B. and Adams, H. B. (1987) 'Assessment and development of potential of high school pupils in the third world context of Kwa Zulu/Natal part 1', *Gifted Educational International* **5**(1), 6–10.

Wallace, B. and Adams, H. B. (1988) 'Assessment and development of potential of high school pupils in the third world context of KwaZulu/Natal part 2', *Gifted Education International* **5**(2), 72–9.

Wallace, B. and Adams, H. B. (eds) (1993a) *Worldwide Perspectives on the Gifted Disadvantaged.* London: AB Academic Publishers.

Wallace, B. and Adams, H. B. (1993b) *TASC Thinking Actively in a Social Context.* London: AB Academic Publishers.

Whitmore, J. R. (1979) 'Identifying and programming for highly gifted underachievers in the elementary school', in Gallagher, J. J. (ed.) *Gifted Children: Reaching their Potential.* Jerusalem: Kollek.

CHAPTER 8

Conclusion

Michael J. Stopper

Summary of key themes

In the introductory chapter we began with, and re-emphasise here, a welcoming of the developing interest in the education of gifted and talented children. However, recognition of the social and emotional underpinning of the educational process is not adequately reflected in current policy-making or provision (nor, sufficiently, within family or community life).

Theoretical constructs of giftedness and talent, which incorporate social and emotional components, have been examined in a brief overview. From these we gain an understanding of skills or 'intelligences' in socio-affective areas which can be developed and that complement and reinforce cognitive abilities.

Since 'need' is a somewhat comfortable and often indiscriminate notion, questions of derivation, assessment and interpretation are considered. There is acknowledgement here of a multi-dimensional concept that includes individual, affiliated and common needs, gender issues, societal demands and expectations and the magnet of peer group identity. The particular challenges faced by those who identify and provide solutions to Mankind's dilemmas and who shape the aesthetic quality of Life – the creatively gifted and talented – are highlighted.

On a final note, there is discussion of needs and wants and their relationship to motivation; and a recommendation for critical reflection regarding goals, the needs themselves and how education (as opposed to other areas of human experience) might fulfil them.

Richard Bentley's chapter on curriculum development and process offers a pressing reminder of the connection between pupil characteristics, needs and provision. Where individual characteristics have been discussed and agreed on, analysis of need has not generally been a natural corollary. Where somewhat greater awareness or understanding exists, this too, is not regularly translated in terms of day-to-day practice. The 'Three Column Model' discussed in Chapter 2, provides a convenient framework for mapping the planning and delivery of carefully matched learning experiences; and the case studies presented validate the model's practical usefulness to teachers.

From the perspective of the seasoned observer, the indicators of a climate for optimal development are given: quality of questioning, metacognitive reflection, emphasis on transfer, parental involvement, problem solving, a strategy menu, and individualised development programmes. Flexibility in both systems and programmes is necessary. It is emphasised that we are not choosing between an emotional and social focus or an intellectual one, but recognising an interdependence that is necessary for successful learning and living. The approaches outlined here can inform practice for all children, but we should note the especial relevance of particular issues to the education of the most able.

As an initial step, schools are encouraged (and provided with the means) to engage in a process of self review – a 'climate audit' (for in asking 'Where do we want to be?' and 'How do we get there?', we must first ask 'Where are we now?'). Current opportunities for all such initiatives now need to be secured.

In advocating ambitious provision for extension and enrichment, Julian Whybra argues strongly for 'true' peer grouping arrangements, i.e. by developmental stages that fully support cognitive, social and emotional needs. Enrichment and extension programmes facilitate such matching. Challenge set through shared experience creates social and intellectual affinity, while accommodating personal fulfilment through individual interests and contact with experts. The commentaries of past attenders of GIFT courses affirm the value of such experience.

The wider implications for mainstream learning include, critically, sensitivity to the demands made by gifted and talented children and the nature of teaching and learning roles.

However, individual teachers function effectively where systems allow creative and flexible responses. Within present frameworks this is not commonplace. Creating a pro-achievement culture across the mainstream peer group remains an insistent challenge. Existing arrangements for supporting talent development in sport and the performing arts suggest a model for promoting academic potential. Also, organisational strategies – flexible timetabling and out of class grouping arrangements that supplement suitably differentiated classroom provision, offer a positive way forward. Cluster and school partnership initiatives allow for shared expertise; premises and resources aid busy teachers; while optimal benefits come from a within-school impetus, effective external provision will provide cues for enhanced teaching and learning. The principles underpinning enrichment and extension again have significant implications for the holistic development of all children.

Susan Gomme's focus on the role of the family echoes the inter-relatedness and parity of social and emotional needs noted earlier. Social need is not the natural precursor of emotional need, which is evident from birth. The subsequent 'emotional input' that the family makes will, therefore, most significantly, be to acknowledge and celebrate a child's unique identity. Resulting social relationships will draw on this recognition (since there are in reality no 'formulas' for raising gifted and talented children). Patterns of future social interaction will be determined by the responses of others to the child's 'differentness' and by the individual's emotional resources. There is an acknowledged sense of vulnerability (rather than fragility) that may be compounded by developmental mismatch in the intellectual, physical, social and emotional domains. Sense of 'belonging' may then be obscured and the security of family life can ease inherent tensions. Lack of correspondence between levels of aspiration and achievement, and between the expectations of others and one's true capability; apparent lack of social skills and absence of emotional affinity and shared interests, put children potentially at risk. Consequently, there is urgent need for properly coordinated liaison and support between, and through, home and school.

A majority of parents may be naturally inclined to encourage talent development by urging persistence and dedication. However, psychological well-being dictates that valuing of the individual should not be overshadowed by valuing of that individual's achievements. Children's self-expectations, exercising of parental responsibility, development of socially appropriate behaviours, sibling relationships, parental aspiration versus individual rights and entitlement and self-fulfilment and 'fitting in', form the template for a family's social and emotional interaction.

The challenges and potentially rich rewards of family life in supporting gifted and talented children and bringing their abilities to fruition, ought to prompt recognition of the support to which parents, too, are entitled.

Lindsay Peer describes an 'invisible disability' that can obscure talent recognition, contribute to a sense of differentness and create social and emotional pressures that undermine motivation and self-esteem. Gifted children with dyslexia lack the advantage of presenting in 'conventional' terms owing to poorer levels of literacy skills than other identified gifted pupils. However, research establishes the reality of highly able visual and creative learners. Building ability profiles through traditional standardised testing is rejected in favour of curriculum based assessment – particularly that extending beyond basic literacy and numeracy skills. Early identification is critical and assessment is now feasible from three years of age.

Increased understanding that giftedness and dyslexia are not mutually exclusive, has not translated to policy and practice. Account should be taken of the distinction between speed of receiving information and speed of processing; and of difficulties with short-term memory, sequencing and laterality. Sensitive and informed teacher response will counteract misinterpretation of ability and commitment. Metacognitive and study skills valuable to all learners are indispensable to gifted dyslexic students; and appropriate monitoring, target setting and learner involvement will reinforce emotional well-being as well as facilitate academic achievement. The 'low emotional ebb' some experience where needs are unrecognised is contrasted when advantage is sometimes taken of strengths to devise coping strategies and achieve notable success.

Remediation of difficulty is essential, but emphasis is placed on developing gifts and talents through specialist support, differentiated materials and classroom practice and access to successful role models. Enhancing self-esteem, maintaining motivation and proactively identifying potential among those with dual exceptionality demand creative resolution.

Under-representation of particular groups in special arrangements for the gifted and talented, is pursued further in Stan Bailey's chapter on the culturally diverse. Identification that neglects the full range of talents within cultural minorities and ill-matched curriculum content and process compound the problem. The central conflict is success as defined by the majority culture at variance with family values and minority norms; the core dilemma – increasing alienation from one's cultural background, yet incomplete integration into mainstream culture.

Schools must develop self-esteem and encourage personal empowerment to function, optimally, in varying ethnic environments at a discretionary level. A cultural interface in learning will include increased parental involvement and understanding; valuing of bilingualism; contact with appropriate role models and mentors; exclusion of stereotypical expectations and sensitive teacher support that fosters emotional security.

Creative use of information and communication technology and bibliotherapy are among additional strategies that promote confidence and build high aspirations. Accommodation of learning style is not exclusive to the culturally diverse, but increased awareness of ethnic cognitive, social and emotional predisposition is warranted. In rejecting deficit-based views and adopting, 'positive, proficiency-orientated' perspectives, a strong case can be made for identification through provision that highlights potential and diagnoses needs. Standardised testing procedures are, consequently, deemed less appropriate than dynamic identification measures. Matched with appropriate expectations and support structures that acknowledge both cultural heritage and individuality, such approaches maximise achievement, avoiding the obstacles that often attend it.

Belle Wallace's theme of social and economic disadvantage is set against the background of a 'humanising education' emerging from the climate in schools and the expectations of society. The social and emotional needs of learners, prioritised within such a curriculum, clearly contribute to high performance.

The respective influences of home and school that combine with an individual's characteristics are examined. In disadvantaged families language development and values acquisition may be inconsistent with school demands and learning culture. Such disparity must be acknowledged and accommodated empathetically.

Parents and teachers should nurture the emotional intelligences: children can be empowered rather than imprisoned by circumstance, through a sense of self-determination and goal-orientated behaviour in particular. Case studies from the writer's own experience reveal the heartening resilience some possess despite constraints upon life chances.

Emergent learner profiles of the disadvantaged commonly feature survival instincts, physical tenacity, practical problem-solving skills and social empathy that provide pathways to enrichment and extension of experience. Low incidence of teacher recognition of high ability in deprived social areas and profiles of under-achievement that resonate with the experience of the disadvantaged, are at contrast with life-enhancing opportunities that the projects described offer. The TASC model (co-developed by the writer with her partner, Harvey Adams) has especial implications for the disadvantaged learner.

Recent government inner-cities initiatives are welcomed but have limitations of scope and vision. Disadvantage clearly demands multi-dimensional educational solutions.

Looking to the future

Briefly, then, what lies ahead in respect of acknowledging and developing social and emotional behaviours and skills that will help gifted and talented children actualise their potential? Passow *et al.* (1993, p. 895) comment: 'As educators become more sensitive to the affective characteristics of the gifted, they will design and adopt educational, counselling and socializing experiences to meet those needs'.

While there are encouraging signs of increased interest and motivation to engage in this area of human development, the education of gifted and talented children is still at a formative stage. There is much that we do not know about the benefits or otherwise of particular approaches; and where research evidence does exist it is often not part of an information interface with teachers and parents. There is a pressing requirement for further study and reflection and for a coherent link between research, policy and practice. Furthermore, as the momentum of the debate increases and far-reaching decisions begin to be made about the needs of the gifted and talented, we ought to pause and consider perhaps the most important perspective of all – the views of the children themselves. We can then, at least, begin to lay claim to having addressed needs as part of the process of meeting them.

Reference

Passow, A. H., Mönks, F. J. and Heller, K. A. (1993) 'Research and education of the gifted in the Year 2000 and beyond', in Heller, A. K., Mönks, F. J. and Passow, A. H. (eds) *International Handbook of Research and Development of Giftedness and Talent.* Oxford: Pergamon Press.

Index